THE LABYRINTHS OF INFORMATION

'Ciborra brings his rich understanding of bricolage and phenomenology to the fore in providing fresh insights about organizations and the building and use of complex information systems. Highly recommended.'

John Seely Brown, former director Xerox PARC;
co-author of *The Social Life of Information*

'Reading Ciborra gives, even to a person who has been in this Industry for many years, a new vision of Information Technology and its impact on organizations and on every human being.'

Elserino Piol, CEO, Pino Venture Capital
(Former Vice-Chairman of Olivetti)

'Ciborra invites us to see through the systems, methods, and boxes of standard organization lore into the buzzing, emotional, and political improvisation in today's networked organizations. He does so to help us make sense of the current uses of information technology. The book is both theoretically more interesting *and* more practical than most writing on the subject. Ciborra is refreshing, original and great fun to read.'

Bo Dahlbom, Director of the Swedish Research Institute
for Information Technology

'Information systems are just the entry point for Claudio Ciborra to take us on a ride through the myths of order and rationality that permeate management practice and dominate our espoused mode of existence. Using powerful metaphors and taking a real and messy world—as opposed to an idealised one—as a starting point, he draws the contours of a higher-level road map. This book is deeply threatening and disturbing in laying bare so many erroneous assumptions and practices, but it ultimately brings a hopeful message. … a must for the next generation of leaders.'

Professor Richard Normann, founder of SMG and
author of *Reframing Business*

'This is a book about how the untidy persists within hi-tech solutions, and about how human improvisation is dynamically related to technical systems. Claudio Ciborra provides us with a compelling analysis that marries an "anthropology of uncertainty" to the understanding of information systems. This brilliant book is a *tour de force* that propels information systems into the heart of the social sciences.'

Henrietta L. Moore, Professor of Social Anthropology, LSE

'Claudio Ciborra has a more detailed, nuanced, and sophisticated understanding of the dynamics associated with information technology in today's organizations than any scholar working in the field today. His work is grounded in ultra realism, but his observations are interpreted through classical schema that provide immense illumination. The effect is a series of highly literate jewel-like essays that are intellectually fascinating but could also change the life of any practitioner who bothered to read and ponder.'

Shoshana Zuboff, Charles Edward Wilson Professor of Business Administration,
Harvard Business School; author of *In the Age of the Smart Machine*

'Knowledge management is not about shopping around for state-of-the-art IT. It is about human beings with differing viewpoints. Ciborra's book … elaborately explains this, and also how we should change our perspectives and attitudes towards information and knowledge in this new century. An excellent book.'

Professor Ikujiro Nonaka, Dean of the Graduate School of Knowledge Science,
JAIST; author of *The Knowledge-Creating Company*

THE LABYRINTHS OF INFORMATION

Challenging the Wisdom of Systems

CLAUDIO CIBORRA

with a Foreword by Professor Kristen Nygaard

OXFORD
UNIVERSITY PRESS

OXFORD

UNIVERSITY PRESS

Great Clarendon Street, Oxford OX2 6DP

Oxford University Press is a department of the University of Oxford.
It furthers the University's objective of excellence in research, scholarship,
and education by publishing worldwide in

Oxford New York

Auckland Bangkok Buenos Aires Cape Town Chennai
Dar es Salaam Delhi Hong Kong Istanbul Karachi Kolkata
Kuala Lumpur Madrid Melbourne Mexico City Mumbai Nairobi
São Paulo Shanghai Singapore Taipei Tokyo Toronto
with an associated company in Berlin

Oxford is a registered trade mark of Oxford University Press
in the UK and in certain other countries

Published in the United States
by Oxford University Press Inc., New York

British Library Cataloguing in Publication Data
Data available

Library of Congress Cataloging in Publication Data
Ciborra, Claudio.
Information complexities : challenging the wisdom of systems / Claudio Ciborra.
p. cm.
Includes bibliographical references and index.
1. Information technology. 2. Technological innovations. 3. Organizational
change. I. Title.
HD30.2 .C53 2002   658.4'038–dc21   2002020185
ISBN 0–19–924152–X

10 9 8 7 6 5 4 3 2 1

Typeset by Newgen Imaging Systems (P) Ltd., Chennai, India
Printed in Great Britain
on acid-free paper by
Biddles Ltd, Guildford and King's Lynn

Foreword

An Emergency Toolkit

This book about system development will, in my opinion, be useful for three main audiences:

- people educated as programmers and system developers and with experience drawn from participating in practical development teams;
- managers and others who have to communicate with such people, benefiting from their efforts or being exposed to the frustrating consequences of their systems;
- researchers and experts in the wide range of fields that, to varying degrees, border or overlap the field of information systems.

It is written by a person who has neither an expert level education nor experience of participation in programming and system development, and who has never been a manager.

The author, Claudio Ciborra—Professor of Information Systems at the London School of Economics and Political Science—has, however, a solid background in management, economics, and organization theory. He has participated in a number of studies of real cases of large-scale system development projects, working closely both with managers and people who have an informatics education. He knows us. This book is an emergency toolkit for us to use in crises; a fairly normal state for our projects.

*

In my opinion our science—informatics—is much broader than the term computer science would restrict it to. It is about phenomena, and should not attempt to become a strictly formal science like mathematics. It deals with *a class of phenomena* and *a set of perspectives* and ways of looking at these phenomena in a similar way to physics, botany, economics, political science and sociology.

Informatics is the science that has *information processes* and *related phenomena* in artefacts, society and nature as its domain.

These *information processes* and *related phenomena* occur in program executions (the physical processes generated in computing equipment when programs are carried out); in the operation of hospital information systems by nurses, doctors, patients, computers, diagnostical equipment; and in the processes of developing, negotiating about, maintaining and modifying systems, to mention a few illustrations.

Sciences are usually described as having three main aspects:

- *Observation*. The empirical study of the phenomena: their identification, observed properties and behaviour.
- *Analysis*. Comprehension and explanation of phenomena in terms of an underlying theory.
- *Synthesis (or construction, technology)*. Knowledge organized for the purpose of designing, generating or modifying phenomena.

There is, however a fourth aspect of sciences.

- *Multiperspective reflection*. The concurrent or alternating use of several perspectives in the consideration of phenomena— perspectives either from within the same science or drawn from more than one science. The study of how changes, introduced according to one viewpoint, affect properties of the phenomena when regarded from another viewpoint.

Observation, analysis and synthesis are standard elements of natural sciences. Multiperspective reflection is not considered so regularly, but it does occur. In the social sciences one often has to deal with conflicting interests. Multiperspective reflection is important, whereas synthesis, 'social engineering', is less prominent. In informatics and operational research both synthesis and multiperspective reflection are essential and are at the core of these sciences. For example, in designing a terminal system for bank tellers, system developers have to apply a system perspective on the set of programs that will enforce correct money-handling procedures upon the tellers' and customers' transactions. They have to apply an economic perspective in their dealings with the bank's chief financial officer; they focus on response times and reducing downtime when dealing with the common interests of tellers and customers; and they consider the need for protection against unwanted social supervision when dealing with the tellers' interests.

The notion of perspective becomes, for these reasons, essential in the science of informatics. It is, however, for any person at any moment an aspect of her or his thinking and relations with the environment. We cannot relate simultaneously to all information available to us, we have to select and make sense of what is selected. The definition I am using is this. In any given *situation*, a person's cognitive process is structured by a *perspective* that:

- is common to a *domain* of situations considered *similar* to the given one;
- *selects those properties* of the situation that are being considered (and, by implication, those that are ignored); and
- *provides concepts and other cognitions* that are being used in the interpretation of the selected properties.

The use of object-oriented programming, 'the most widely used programming model today',[1] implies that an information process is regarded as a system. What does that mean? What *is* a system? A system developer should be careful when using the verb *to be*. Nothing is *inherently* a system, but we may state that part of the world is a system to us when we study it using a *system perspective*.

A *system* is a part of the world that is regarded as a whole with:

- its *substance* consisting of *components*;
- each component's *state* characterized by the states of *properties*, called *attributes*, that are *selected* as being relevant; and by
- *state transitions* relating to these attributes and to other components and their attributes.

In object-oriented programming all substance components (the physical matter participating in a program execution, such as records, files, variables, and so on) are organized as objects. Any property of the system is the property of one, and only one, of these objects. All action carried out in the system is carried out by objects. Most programs that are written and used thus embed a system perspective, and it becomes meaningless to state that one 'is against' this perspective. There is, however, much more to consider in information system development than what one may usefully capture by a system perspective, and within a system perspective many different approaches are possible.

When a chemical factory asks for tenders for delivery of a specified chemical, the products offered by suppliers as satisfying the specifications may have been produced by completely different processes. The same may be true in the supply of cogwheels.

---

[1] Association for Computing Machinery (ACM) press release 5 Feb. 2002, issued in New York.

In contrast, the properties of a complex information system are rarely independent of the processes by which it has been produced. The methods used in such system development processes always embed social perspectives on values; on the power structure of the organization carrying out the process; on how to treat conflicts; and so on. These perspectives are usually not made explicit; probably it has never occurred to those who designed the methods that they ought to do this.

The most common deficiency of system development methods is that they fail to identify the actors and other persons or groups who have vested interests in the system and its development process. In a societal situation, such notions as *values, interests, power* are unavoidable elements. Knowledge based systems will be designed, and later manipulated by opposing actors, as tools to achieve contested goals, regardless of the stated and/or intended purpose of these systems. It also should be remembered that in many social situations *moods* and *affections* may play an important role.

It is a common experience in system development case studies that events reported by participants do not, upon closer scrutiny, correspond to what happened. Important events and relationships are overlooked or hidden. Why? On many occasions, the method the developer attempted (or was instructed) to use did not work in practice, but still was reported as having been used. Other times, crucial actual events were overlooked or misinterpreted because a more suitable perspective for understanding the situation at hand was lacking; crises could not be explained and dealt with properly.

Claudio Ciborra's book addresses these situations that regularly confront the system developers and their organizational environment. He has a series of alternative perspectives and insights to offer. It is not necessary to accept all, or any, of these perspectives as 'correct' or as closely covering the problem at hand. The book has served its purpose if it opens your mind, makes you a keener observer, provides you with some new tools for crisis management, or, better still, for steering you away from crises. *No single perspective is sufficient when one is considering the development and use of an information system.*

Henrietta L. Moore, Professor of Social Anthropology at LSE has said that, 'this brilliant book is a *tour de force* that propels information systems into the heart of the social sciences'. I agree, and only want to add that the study of information systems in their social and organizational context remains at the heart of the discipline of informatics.

Kristen Nygaard

Kristen Nygaard is Professor (emeritus) at the Department of Informatics at the University of Oslo, Norway. He is, together with Ole-Johan Dahl, the inventor of the Simula languages and thus of object-oriented programming. He has been doing research on societal implications of ICT, on ICT seen from the perspectives of Trade Unions, and he is regarded as the founder of the 'Scandinavian School' of systems development. He has (together with Ole-Johan Dahl) received the IEEE John von Neumann Medal and the ACM Alan M. Turing Award, and been named Commander of the Order of Saint Olav by the King of Norway.

Acknowledgements

My thanks go to those cities, companies, and universities, researchers, colleagues, and friends who have hosted me during the gyrations of my pilgrimage; in particular the Department of Information Systems at the LSE.

And special thanks to those who in various capacities worked on the manuscript: Mike Cushman, Emma Peel, and Daniel Osei-Joehene at the LSE, and David Musson, Sarah Dobson, and Jackie Pritchard at OUP.

Contents

Figure

Tables

Abbreviations

AHS	American Hospital Supply
AI	Artificial Intelligence
B2B	Business to Business
B2C	Business to Customers
BCG	Boston Consulting Group
BPR	Business Process Re-engineering
CASE	Computer-Aided Software Engineering
CMM	Capability Maturity Model
CRM	Customer Relationship Management
DGT	Direction Générale des Télécommunications
ERP	Enterprise Resource Planning
GDSS	Group Decision Support Systems
ICT	Information and Communication Technology
IS	Information System
ISO	International Standards Organization
MIS	Management Information System
OEM	Original Equipment Manufacturer
PC	Personal Computer
PTT	Post, Telegraph, and Telephones
RISC	Reduced Instruction Set Computer
SIS	Strategic Information System

1

Invitation

The current descriptions of the design, implementation, management, and use of information technology in organizations (in short information systems) are largely founded on notions of rationality, science, and method. This is probably because the initial diffusion of business applications of computers and networks, and the highly formalized nature of programming and software, suggested a vigorous and structured understanding and representation of the multiple systems practices, from requirement analysis to use, maintenance, and documentation.

The essays in this volume attempt to engage the reader in thinking and articulating his or her practices otherwise. By covering key topics, such as systems development, strategic alignment, or change management, they put forward a significant shift from the scientific paradigm that looms large over the multiple facets of the introduction and use of information and communication technology (ICT) in organizations. In particular they point to an alternative centre of gravity: human existence in everyday life.

Such a Copernican revolution is accomplished first by unveiling the hidden or dark side of information systems, or, to put it differently, focusing on the obvious, the workaday, and the very well known to any practitioner in the field. These are events, episodes, practices, and related narratives seldom hosted in the neat representations of systems, data flows, processes, entities, and relationships; rather they are made popular by the swapping of war stories among practitioners. Indeed, activities such as hacking, improvising, tinkering, applying patches, and cutting corners seem to punctuate ubiquitously the everyday life of systems.

We are going to explore and value in relation to information systems such ordinary phenomena, which can be found in the development and use of any complex technical system. A good example is the adventurous (and long) life of the Russian MIR space station. Up there, revolving in space, one could find, hand in hand, advanced, robust engineering solutions, rustic design, and widespread virtuoso tinkering (what the French call *bricolage*) to keep the equipment and the system going as a whole. MIR has been a staccato technology, able to defy the passing of time, the inevitable downgrading of performance, and major and minor breakdowns, providing another opportunity for all to see the approximations of science and technology in use.

Most of the successful, or even strategic, ICT applications in organizations resemble, if one just scratches the glossy surface of the official presentation slides, staccato high-tech space stations. Hence the idea to write a book on information systems that celebrates these practices, looks at their impacts, and discovers the relevant human skills, which may turn out to be key factors permeating any high-tech setting.

Multiple research projects, both empirical and conceptual, have convinced me of the need to be more attentive to the importance of the unfinished, the untidy, the irregular, and the hack as fundamental systems practices.

The discovery of the (functional) power of the improvised and trumped up—that which is anathema to prevailing software engineering models and methods, even to those more oriented to professions or people—has been an important outcome of the study of actual people's roles in taking care of complex information systems. The investigations were carried out in the original spirit of socio-technical research, considering carefully the interaction between the engineering detail of the technical systems and the related dynamics of the surrounding social arrangements. The debate in the strategic management literature (in particular the resource-based view of strategy) has also helped me to focus on the key role of those soft or ad-hoc technology-related practices that can be the source of competitive advantage.

What does one do with the consistent empirical discovery of the approximate and happenstance nature of systems and methods once they get implemented? A first task for the academic is to present results and test new ideas through scientific publications and university seminars.[1] Also, a more domesticated (i.e. less pointedly academic) version of the findings and issues becomes the object of debate at advanced executive seminars and lectures.

To be sure, feedback on the discoveries over the years has been rather comforting and a certain interest has been raised in the academic community (and a niche created in the cacophony of information systems studies). But out of all these places, the real

---

[1] The seven chapters that follow are based on previous academic publications by the author. Sources for the original versions are given on the first page of each chapter.

impetus, from which the idea of this book originally took shape, has occurred during the executive seminars, where things have often tended to escalate. Indeed, reactions to the findings and new ideas have been red-hot, whether in favour or against. Seminars have never ended on a neutral tone. It has been either 'Great, finally a speaker who understands us!' or 'Never, never call him back again'.

The subjects of the seminars and of this book, ranging from corporate information infrastructures to organizational and strategic alignment, are usually seen to verge on the boring and not capable of triggering vehement reactions of any sort. Still, excited debate and strong disagreement have often been the case and my conclusion is that the animal spirits of managers and specialists seem to resonate well to the contents of the seminars. Why is this so?

One possible explanation of the controversies is the mixed signals emanating from the sessions. On the one hand the everyday experience is evoked: the ubiquitous muddling through to get systems implemented and used. On the other hand, precisely because this kind of experience is well known and shared, specialists and managers do not want to hear about it, especially from an academic, and would rather focus on prospects of improved models and methods.

Interestingly enough, no matter what the specific contents of the discussion or the teaching were, one could feel in a distinct, albeit implicit way that, on certain approaches or issues, the participants reached a different level of awareness through their efforts to understand, discuss, and reflect. This had not much to do with the relevance of the case studies, the slickness of the presentation, or the novelty of the theory. At a moment of truth, participants felt that at stake was not just the information infrastructure, the re-engineering of processes, or their own organizational problems: it was they themselves, there, in class, arguing, reflecting, being puzzled, feeling let down, reminded of their unsolvable messes back home.

Thus, I began to play with the idea that even when discussing decision making, transaction costs, knowledge management, or enterprise resource planning applications, there must be an authentic and an inauthentic way to deal with these issues. I submit that the former way feeds upon something that is beyond technology, management, and organization, but that contributes to put all these things into action: those participants being there in the session with their personal histories, problems, projects, visions, and disillusions. What is at stake in those situations is who they are, where they come from professionally and person-ally, and towards what they are projected in relation to the issues raised by the speaker. Although the issues are well known, the magic may be the speaker, who, as an outside observer, dares to enquire publicly into them.

My aim in this book is to provide a first catalogue of ideas and dilemmas similar to those that have fuelled the debate in the exec-utive seminars. The topics and the preoccupations at its core revolve around strategy, technological innovation, systems devel-opment, organizational design, and change. But their treatment is different. No matter how practical or business oriented the current management and systems literatures on these and related topics are, they tend to rely, for reasons of legitimacy and credibility, on *methods* that are simple, rational, and, especially, based on the natural science paradigm. Unfortunately, the scientific method is based on a peculiar way of understanding the world: a world represented as an ensemble of entities, objects, and people. But such understanding does not support us in the way we normally encounter (and learn to know) the world: by dealing with it as a set of interdependent tools. In this respect, science-based, method-driven approaches can be misleading. Contrary to their promise, they are deceivingly abstract and removed from practice. Everyone can experience this when he or she moves from the models to the implementation phase. The words of caution and the pleas for 'change management' interventions that usually accompany the sophisticated methods and polished models keep reminding us of such an implementation gap. However, they offer no valid clue on how to overcome it, only another procedural sequence of steps and phases that in its turn will require a further bridging between the method and the concrete situation.

How to get closer to practice, then, and the real life of systems in use in a fresher way? Let us start by realizing that our involvement with systems is driven by an anticipating, mood-affected vision that relentlessly navigates, discovers, and encounters the world. Understanding is grounded on this human attitude of being open to possibilities and continuous caring about events, resources, behaviours, and problems. Such an attitude is the engine behind those informal practices referred to above: *bricolage*, hacking, and improvisation. This is the domain of existing in the world. Hence, a different perspective on information systems should be anchored to the unfolding of the human process of encountering the everyday world.

Indeed, one way to get closer to the obvious which permeates the everyday chores is first to put aside all our concerns for methods and scientific modelling and encounter the multiple apparitions through which strategizing, knowing, organizing, and implementing offer themselves to our relentless, mood-affected caring for, and dealing with, the world. As a help in this direction the reader will find each of the chapters introduced by a title, a non-English word, aimed at creating an uncanny dislocation of perspective, suspending, if only for a brief instant, his or her usual attitude and expectations.

At the end of the volume a Methodological Appendix makes explicit the style of phenomenological understanding that underlies the seven essays. It illustrates how to go beyond appearances and the illusionary realness of those management and systems concepts in common currency and how to value the apparitions of the ordinary in the life of information systems and organizations.

To be sure, the themes discussed in this book need not stay confined within the limits of the profession and academic discipline of information systems. It is imperative to appreciate the ideas contained in the chapters in a broader perspective; after all, the field of information systems deals with the deployment of information technology in organizations, institutions, and society at large. This is the context of the information society, characterized by ubiquitous information infrastructures, as well as by processes of globalization, networking, increasing speed of economic transactions, and rapid social transformation.

In particular, the global dynamics we are confronted with are the ones of the increasing quantities of knowledge embedded in systems and shared between organizations and individuals; the increased transparency and interdependence that the new systems bring about, and hence the higher level of risk for systems, individuals, and institutions when breakdowns do occur. Last but not least, there is the awareness according to which the unavoidable side effects and the denser knowledge inputs to systems and processes force us to address new problems and learn new things. Learning by individuals, groups, and organizations, and their ensuing ability to reflect and to create new knowledge, are, in their turn, factors that permit the information society to evolve, the world to run faster, and simultaneously decrease our chances of effective control and governance given their higher levels of complexity.

If these are some of the salient traits of our high-tech, modern world, a new light is cast on questions related to what to do and how to operate in organizations and within technological platforms dominated by side effects; in situations where, by definition, resources and people are not fully under control, and where any new system or method we apply in order to perfect our management capabilities is condemned to be yet a new source of unexpected consequences. In particular, the emphasis placed on such mundane activities as improvisation and *bricolage*, often reputed to be marginal when dealing with high-tech milieux, appears to be dictated by a renewed concern not only for human existence as a neglected factor in the implementation of complex systems and organizations, but also, normatively, for those (sometimes age-old) skills and competencies required for living in a runaway world driven by spiralling side effects.

Let me conclude with an analogy that may help to spell out the main thrust behind the attempt at redefining the agenda of information systems design, development, and management as put forward in the book. The analogy is with the history of the arts in the fifteenth century. Renaissance painters accomplished a great formal revolution (relative to medieval art) by reaching new levels of realism in portraying human figures, landscapes, and buildings (think of the works of Raphael). However, the human figures in Renaissance paintings are highly classical and extremely idealized: ideal men and women were at the centre of the artistic representations. A century later, Italian Baroque painters and the Dutch painters of the Golden Age were able to carry out another dramatic revolution by introducing two key elements: the celebration of everyday life, instead of classical or religious themes, (think of Vermeer) and the representation of emotions and moods in the human figure (think of Caravaggio). Simultaneously, the same revolution was taking place in the world of music: from polyphonic harmony ruled by the perfection of mathematical proportions in the music of the Middle Ages and the Renaissance to the tears that moved audiences during the first performances of Monteverdi's *Lamento d'Arianna* in 1608.

I suggest that the information systems field, with its rational views of knowledge, decision making, strategy, and orderly systems development, is based on a narrow model of rational, ideal actors. In this book, by focusing on the mundane and the existential, I want to contribute to a transition of the field towards an Age of the Baroque in the deployment and management of technology in organizations and society. Passion and improvisation; moods and *bricolage*; emotions and workaday chores; existence and procedures will become integral to systems design and use, casting new shadows and lights on the unfolding world of technology.

2

Krisis

> Briefly, my case is this: I've completely lost the ability to
> think or speak coherently about anything . . . The abstract
> words which the tongue has to employ in order to express
> any kind of daily opinion decompose in my mouth like
> rotten mushrooms.
>
> (Hugo von Hofmannsthal, letter to Lord Chandos)

It may indeed sound bizarre to talk about a crisis. There seem to
be very few signs to this effect. Companies are busy seeking strategic applications of ICTs, savouring the delights and pitfalls of
more and more sophisticated networks; they are experimenting
with groupware applications and Intranets; they are re-engineering
and re-inventing multiple processes, ranging from customer
relationship to international business and training . . . always

This chapter is based on two papers: C. U. Ciborra (1997), '*De profundis?*
Deconstructing the concept of strategic alignment', *Scandinavian Journal of
Information Systems*, 91: 67–82; C. U. Ciborra (1998), 'Crisis and foundations: an
inquiry into the nature and limits of models and methods in the information
systems discipline', *Journal of Strategic Information Systems*, 7: 5–16.

with ICT. All these activities, and many others, create a demand for new information systems (IS) specialists, ranging from the more technically to the more business-oriented ones. This has in turn created a very favourable climate for academic opportunities: from professorial chairs to Ph.D. positions. So why should one think about a 'crisis' in IS, or even the possibility of one? Framed in these terms, the question is totally unwarranted and untimely, for the crisis occurred some time ago and simply remains with us. In this respect, there is not a *new* crisis in sight, at least in the short to medium term. But, then, how can we experience simultaneously both crisis and success?

My tentative answer is the following: the success due to the growing number and increasing variety of ICT applications—pulling in its wake the demand for more education, research, and academic resources—has occurred *despite* the contents, directions, trends, and main characteristics of the ICT-related disciplines, in particular the IS one. I know that many of you know exactly what I am talking about, but for those who do not, and those who may resist saying out loud what they tacitly acknowledge, let me recall some 'paradigmatic cases'.

Strategic applications of ICT, to begin with, came before any textbook or article in our disciplines talked about them (see the next chapter). While specialists and managers in American Airlines and McKesson were tinkering and developing strategic applications by linking customers or suppliers through electronic networks, in most 1970s textbooks 'strategic' was a label to be attached only to exotic, Artificial Intelligence (AI) based applications aimed at supporting decision making at the top of the organization. None of these systems ever saw the light of the day, and the ambitions of AI itself have been severely curbed, while 'bread and butter' order entry systems were tilting the balance of entire industries in favour of pioneering firms adopting them.

Let me turn the knife deeper in the (academic) wound: the Internet, the current phenomenon that has boosted a renewed interest in the IS curricula, emerged, as a concept, as a technology, and as a set of applications, totally outside our field. Disturbingly, it shows a number of features that fly directly in the face of what used to be found in the typical Management Information Systems (MIS) textbook. The Internet is about horizontal networking, while in many textbooks you can still see a (closed) pyramid representing the firm and its corresponding information system. The Internet has emerged as a flexible infrastructure outside any strategic master plan; it allows people to share knowledge in ways our textbooks had not even imagined, where knowledge meant expert systems only. Additionally, it has defeated all the standards defined by ISO and similar committees.

Next, consider systems analysis and design methodologies. Much IS teaching is about methodologies: from structured ones with computer-aided tools (CASE) supporting them, to business redesign methodologies like Business Process Re-engineering (BPR). The core, if not the identity, of our discipline has been revolving around such methodologies, or possibly, as I will argue below, around the very idea of method itself. Still we seem to be devoting much teaching (and consultancy) to something which, to be generous, fails at least half the time. Systems design methods may be the most diffused tools on earth ever to accompany the introduction of a new technology, but they work only in part. There are various signs of this: major systems failures where the methodology has not been able to rescue the project; long delays and sky-rocketing costs of many applications, despite the use of methodologies; the alarming two-thirds failure rate of BPR initiatives; a level of effectiveness of CASE tools far below the one promised and expected; the design and implementation of complex programs like Linux in ways that do not comply with most of the tenets of the structured methodologies; and finally the related emergence of alternative software practices like 'extreme programming'.

To me, such paradigmatic examples suggest that we should not be too proud of our current success and, moreover, that a frank gaze into a mirror placed in front of our discipline should convince us that we actually are in a crisis that started some time ago.

A phenomenological understanding

Crises are somehow connected to forgetting. Let us engage in an exercise of recollection as an attempt to seek new foundations for a way out of the crisis. More than sixty years ago the founder of phenomenology, Edmund Husserl, addressed, in a series of lectures and conferences, the issue of the 'Crisis of European Sciences and Transcendental Phenomenology' in a way that is highly relevant for the (forgotten) dilemmas our discipline has been facing lately. To be sure, speaking in 1934 about the lack of foundation in the sciences, the gap between scientific objectivity and the everyday life world, the lack of a 'spiritual' dimension in technological advancement that may lead to disaster, the undermining of the practical ideal of Europe based on a rational spirit, and the choice facing the West between barbarism and a deep spiritual renewal makes those lectures highly prophetic, considering what happened in Europe and across the world soon after. Here, we will revisit some of Husserl's ideas and arguments with a much more modest intent. The way he talks about science and method (at that time successful but currently in crisis in IS), his analysis of the origins and motives of the crisis, his way of dealing with the trade-offs between objectivity and subjectivity in the sciences, his insightful reflection upon the emergence of the modern scientific method, and, critically, the central and foundational role played by everyday life practices offer a number of new insights into, and hints on how to go about, the strange mixture of latent crisis and apparent success we are confronting in our discipline. In its original meaning, the Greek word *krisis* implies a pulling apart, a separating. In our case, two separations are at work: there is an original separation of something from something else and there is the moving away from the original separation, a forgetfulness. Indeed, it is only by forgetting the crisis that we can live with success in a sort of business-as-usual fashion.

Specifically, following Husserl's analysis, the crisis comes about due to the separation between people and science, and the ensuing forgetting of issues such as the subjective origin of science, the foundational role of everyday life in the creation and development of any methodology, and, ultimately, the obliterating of authentic human existence in the management of organizations and technologies.

The IS discipline, being hybrid and dealing with socio-technical hybrids, is hard to classify as a natural or a human science. The very definition of information systems as a set of technical (scientific) and human resources devoted to the management of information in organizations spells out the composite nature of the field. The same could apply to the well-known definition of information as data—physical or logical signs (natural-scientific)—endowed with interpretation by a user (human or social-scientific). What concerns us here is not the distinction between natural and human sciences *per se*. It is that despite the hybrid, and at limit ambiguous, nature of the problem, a common, unified paradigm has been adopted across the board to deal with its human and natural dimensions: the paradigm of the natural sciences and the collateral methodologies of measurement, formalization, and calculation (of course, this tends to be true for management 'science' in general).

Natural sciences proceed by describing nature on the basis of observation of empirical facts. They provide and order such facts, to make claims to discovering the essential laws of causality connecting the spatio-temporal facts yielded by observation. They proclaim themselves to be objective: that is, they can describe the essence of nature as it is, regardless of the subject. This objectivity determines the procedure or method by which they proceed: the world gets experienced as an object. Within the IS field most of the consultants and academic experts try to adopt, extend, and sometime mimic the natural science way of proceeding, stumbling, however, upon some aberrations. For example, social systems, like business organizations, are observed and analysed in the same fashion—even using the same means of representation—as the physical systems (the computer) or the quasi-mathematical abstractions of the data flows or entity-relationship graphs.

Thus, one tends to forget both the role of human choice behind the technical artefacts, and study the user side of information systems by adopting the methods of the natural sciences.

It is certainly true that today there is a richer stock of research results and publications of a more qualitative nature, thanks to ethnographies, case studies, and concern for the social aspects of computing. Still, such qualitative material is confined at the margins of many educational programmes in engineering and business schools, at least for the time being. Moreover, there is something subtle and troubling. Reflect on the following: in order to show that structured methodologies are a failure or plainly are not used, one is required to adopt a structured, scientific method to empirically measure the phenomenon, otherwise one is neither credible nor legitimate to the mainstream audience; and even then, being methodologies at the core of our discipline, these empirically measured findings are still dismissed. If a new routine invoked to correct or change a pre-existing routine still shows the same problematic features, it means that both are shaped by the same formative context (Ciborra and Lanzara 1994) and share those same traits that lie at the core of such a context. In our case, the preoccupation with method is present even when we question the efficacy of methodologies. Hence, *concern with method is probably one of the key aspects of our discipline, and possibly the true origin of its crisis.*

Against method

Husserl identifies in Galileo the 'discovering and concealing genius' at the origin of the modern scientific attitude and its crisis. Galileo made significant advances in perfecting the scientific approach and transformed it into a methodology, subsequently generalized by Descartes. These advances comprised joining the procedures of abstraction and formalization (already known from the time of the ancient Greeks) with a special sort of idealization, geometry. Husserl points to a subtle transformation carried out by the scientific method. Geometry first uses ideal shapes as approximations of the vague shapes that exist in nature, for both description and manipulation purposes; next, we grant to such ideal entities essence and existence; then they come, almost imperceptibly, to be seen no longer as useful approximations, but as saying something that is true about nature itself; eventually, ideal entities are substituted for reality, and the vague contours of the everyday reality and the human subjects who move around it are dismissed or simply forgotten. A further important step of this process is the arithmetization of geometry. The actual geometric forms are measured and transformed into pure, numerical idealities. And, thanks to a further shift, such pure idealities come to be seen as the way nature really is in itself and should be discovered. As Galileo states in a famous passage, the book of the universe lies open in front of our eyes. We can understand it using the language and the alphabet in which it is composed: those of mathematics and geometry. Otherwise we are left wandering in a dark labyrinth.

The transformation brought about by Galileo conceals a fundamental methodological distortion or inversion. We live and operate in a life world that has vague and murky contours. We might not like it, but this everyday reality, with all its imperfections and unpredictabilities, is real, while it is the outcomes of abstraction and mathematization that are ideal. With Husserl, I submit that we should abolish, or at least suspend, the belief that behind the messy everyday reality there is a geometric universe (maybe like the one provided by virtual reality helmets!). But it is the inverse that occurs: it is the messy life world in which the engineer and wannabe Galilean social scientist live that is fundamental, in the sense that it grounds the abstractions and idealities and lets them become understood and appreciated.

Disciplines such as ours that are inspired by the paradigm of the Galilean method tend to disregard the fundamental role of the everyday life world of the agents, users, designers, and managers, and the messiness and situatedness of their acting, while privileging the geometric worlds created by system methodologies. In this way, the key element is neglected: human existence, which represents the essential ingredient of what information is, of how the life world gets encountered, defined, and reshuffled.

Ironically, if one lesson can be extracted from the major developments that are sustaining the current success of our discipline, it is the strategic importance of ordinary modes of operation, such as *bricolage*, heuristics, serendipity, make-do, rather than the idealities of methods (see the next chapter). But our concern and preoccupation with method is so deeply entrenched that we remain blind to such strong empirical reminders.

Two cases

We can consider two models in common use as examples of the pervasive impact of the Galilean approach on our field: the capability maturity model (CMM) in the software development field, and the model of strategic alignment in the business and ICT strategy arena. Despite the distance between them in terms of application domains, they deal with routine approaches belonging to the same formative context underpinned by the scientific paradigm. BPR has not been selected as an example, given its incredible mélange of propaganda, ideology, and method. Its high failure rate is the sort of empirical evidence that excludes such an approach from having anything to do with a sound methodology at all.

Far from being a mechanistic or Tayloristic methodology as are many of the structured ones coming from software engin- eering, CMM is aimed at improving software processes, thanks to an approach that is incremental and learning oriented. On closer inspection, however, it can be seen that learning and improvement take place within a strict scientific and engineering mindset. The software process, in order to be improved, has to be rendered predictable and to proceed according to plan. Specifically, the process has to be made stable and placed under control through techniques of statistical process control, so that its behaviour is predictable within established statistical limits. Underlying this approach is an emphasis on measurement. 'If you cannot measure it (i.e. express it in numbers) you do not know it, hence you cannot control it,' keep repeating the specialists. CMM is based on benchmarking the current organization of software production against an ideal model that includes five maturity stages, ranging from an initial, rather chaotic stage up to an optimizing stage. Benchmarking requires detailed measurement procedures and techniques. A closer look at the prescriptions of how to measure software processes would reveal the mismatch or even the clash between emphasis on scientific measures based on abstraction and formalization and the multiple social aspects of software production. There are plenty of difficulties and dilemmas in trying to standardize the main features of the complex life world of software: measurement interferes with the specialists' work; questionnaires are based on subjective evaluations; unpredictable events may disrupt the auditing process; the measurement apparatus entails an overhead that small innovative organizations or project teams cannot afford; moving incrementally along the stages may imply unrealistic lengths of time; organizations that want to experiment may intentionally stretch the use of tools and ideas from another stage, and learn from the mistakes . . .

Watch the subtle shift. There is tension between the ideal, the measurement techniques that should locate the messy life world within the model, and the various actions that should be taken to make the life world of the software organization conform to the model. The instrumental and abstract role of the CMM organization is forgotten. Instead, the ideal model is taken as self-evidently describing the evolution of the software organization 'as it is in itself'. Hence, the software specialists are induced to push their organization along the prescribed learning curve. Good performance requires strict adherence to the methodological steps, regardless of circumstances: even in a learning-oriented methodology the abstract model and the related measurements come to dictate human behaviour, up to the point that leading software experts admit that CMM with its bias for 'technologies of reason' needs to be supplemented with a proper concern for experimentation (or tinkering) and true organizational learning.

Secondly, we can look at the issue of strategic alignment between business organizations and ICT. Strategic alignment has been defined as the inherently dynamic fit between external and internal business domains, such as the product/market, strategy, administrative structures, business processes, and ICT. Business performance is seen to be enhanced by finding the right fit between external positioning and internal arrangements. Research on strategic alignment has drawn a badly needed connecting line between strategy, ICT master plans, and business processes and structures.

We should reflect upon what management and IS scholars have done with this idea and the related research programme. They have taken the concepts of strategy and technology for granted, they have quickly blackboxed them and drawn a bridging line between them. Next they started to measure the linkages in the out-there business world. I submit, rather, that alignment often does not obtain, and that the research programme has collapsed since those very concepts should have been taken not for granted, but as problematic. Ethnographic research about the implementation and use of information technology suggests that quite often even in large organizations:

- leadership is missing; and
- the technology is drifting, as if out of control.

The question is, then, how come researchers privilege the geometry of the line connecting abstract concepts in a model, while they remain blind to the blurred reality that any, even slight, ethnographic study would have revealed?

Here we re-encounter the general problem of the relationship between management models and methods (and their geometric representations, with lines and boxes), and everyday phenomena concerning the existence of people at work. We ask: what happens when we link the boxes of strategy, organization, and IT on a diamond diagram *à la* The Corporation of the 1990s (Scott Morton 1991)? It changes our representation of the interdependencies between some key business variables. We obtain a new geometric representation that materializes the idea of alignment in front of our eyes. Thanks to such representation we can spread the news and raise the awareness of managers, simply by showing them the diagram, as a reminder of a more effective map with which to venture into the world of business.

We can ask further: how do these (newly traced) geometrical lines translate into a new management behaviour and improved performance? This question is pertinent, since awareness, or espoused theories, are not enough to learn new behaviour. Indeed, despite the research discovery and its translation into new management models, the news from the field is that alignment is not easy to implement, awareness does not suffice, and the main poles of alignment: strategy and technology are drifting away for one reason or another (see Chapter 5).

A representation which does not work, or which does not deliver as promised, provokes a breakdown, and through this breakdown we (at last) encounter the world, possibly with different eyes. Indeed, the grey world of organizations, always there with its pasted up sets of arrangements, people, and machines which are not aligned according to our models, reminds us of Galileo's method. While focusing on the geometrical representations of business variables and interdependencies we tend to grant them essence and existence: it is an ideal, perfect world to which any real world has to conform. Thanks to a careful and rigorous research method smart researchers discover the ideal, objective world and then they extract the relevant models; effective managers steer the real world towards the models, once they have learnt them. I would argue that it is precisely this belief that is the source of breakdowns, deadlocks, and ultimately impotence.

Let us take a closer look at the research and methodology development process: the messy world that we encounter daily—already there, largely outside our control, and that we know by pre-scientific evidence and intuition—provides us with the raw materials for our abstract representations. We intentionally take the raw materials, we sanitize them, elicit (through some measurement method) a limited number of connections, and build models by fitting in empirical data. However sophisticated they may become, such models remain an image of the organization outside of its world. They are granted essence and existence in the domain of abstractions. Outside that domain they are simply not indexed by the same degree of reality of the world-out-there. We can understand the very notion of alignment only thanks to our (tacit) knowledge of the messy world. But the reverse relationship does not hold true: starting from the notion of alignment, we have difficulties in reconstructing, or intervening in, the messy world of business.

As Husserl points out, we tend to apprehend and explain the world with the help of categories that claim to define it objectively as a set of given objects and relationships, existing in themselves and capable of being grasped by exact measurement methods. For example, we come to believe that alignment (or lack of it) is out there, and that we need to measure it more exactly, so that we will then be able to re-engineer it.

But such a would-be scientific view of the world is one among many, the outcome of the practice of a sub-community of specialists. *The world-out-there is the precondition for our understanding of such models and methods; thus it presupposes them, and is far from being presupposed by them.*

Translated into our case, there is no pure alignment to be measured out there. It is on the contrary our pre-scientific understanding of, and our participation in, the world of organizations that gives to the notion of alignment a shaky and ephemeral existence as an abstraction in our discourses and representations. We need to regard the geometrical models as an (often dogmatic) superstructure world, as an outcome of an idealization process. But in order to reach for the raw materials of what has been idealized we need to go back to the foundation of the superstructure: the life world and the immediate evidence from our experience.

We can now explain the trajectory of the failed research programme on strategic alignment: researchers have made multiple abstractions out of muddling through and drifting; idealized tinkering and called it strategy; idealized technology as a controllable set of means and called it ICT; and granted to these concepts existence and essence, transformed them into boxes and traced a line between them. Then, they have started the difficult journey back to the real world, and found difficulties in measuring the strength of this line or formulating prescriptions that would be followed by managers when tracing this line on the field of practice. They have ingeniously provided more and more sophisticated representations of alignment, as more analytical and detailed maps for the actors to operate in the real world. All this effort is to no avail: the higher conceptual detail has remained confined to the domain of idealized abstractions, with little or no impact on the life world of business and organizations.

A different tack

We can envisage an alternative approach to overcome the crisis generated by an overdose of methodologies. Let us go back to the basics and encounter the world as it presents itself in our everyday experience. We rely on evidence, intuition, and empathy. We listen to managers and we participate in their dealings with puzzles and riddles, and, on the other hand, we do not confer any particular relevance on words like 'strategy', 'processes', 'data', 'system', or 'structured methodology'. In so doing, putting into brackets as it were the models and methods of management science, we approach the everyday life of the manager, made up of frustrations, accomplishments, gossip, confusion, tinkering, joy, and desperation. We are more than discouraged: this is just the everyday world we already live in. We turn to the door of management science to escape towards an objective and reified world, and we find the door locked by our new methodological choice. We are stuck. Can we come up with any sense of this blurred environment and address some of the issues raised so far?

For example, if we listen to the everyday conversations of managers we do hear the familiar terms of strategy, product/markets, and even alignment of systems and administrative structures. They can be interviewed on such topics, and some of their statements even lead to measurements on a Likert scale. But, beyond their espoused views, we can observe such phenomena as: plans that keep being diverted, surprises that arise constantly, opportunistic adjustments that must be carried out on the spur of the moment. We see that, although planning is espoused, circumstances compel managers to improvise, and the implementation of the technology, too, is punctuated by unexpected outcomes and turns that require frequent adaptations if not re-inventions of the initial system.

At this point we are again confronted with a choice. Either we do what management science suggests, that is, idealize from these surprises in implementation, build an ideal world of 'how things should be', and try to operate in such a way that the messy reality in which managers operate moves towards this model (where surprises are absent or under control), or we keep on putting into brackets what we believe we know about strategy, structure, markets, feedback mechanisms, stage curves, and so on, and reflect upon what we observe. We accept coexistence with the messiness of the worldly routines and surprises without panicking.

Sticking to the latter tack, we encounter business phenomena that deeply enrich our geometric notions of organization and technology: consider the chapters that follow as a Baedeker.

Finally, though I am convinced, as are other scholars in the field, that a thorough critique of methodologies and the scientific method as the leading way to automate organizations is a very valuable and refreshing means for our discipline to overcome its latent crisis, I have also gained the impression that this might be only a temporary or intermediate goal. Our concern for methods stands for something even more fundamental. What calls us to devise methodologies? Possibly it is technology itself, and its enframing effect (see Chapter 4). Methods can be regarded as the language in which technology has spoken to us through specialized human agents, such as designers and developers. That most systems analysis methodologies were originally used to represent data flowing in the machines, then being applied to describing organizations, but still with the same representations, seems to support such an idea. Newer systems, such as strategic information systems, the Internet, and the emergence of global ICT infrastructures, all seem to suggest that today technology may require us to speak another language, less formal and structured, more fragmented and oriented to recombination (object orientation may be read as a sign in this direction). We have had the illusion of being modern by trusting structured methodologies. Possibly, we are beginning to realize that they are too naïve and do not capture the intricacies of everyday life: the next challenge for ubiquitous and invisible computing. The plea of this book can then be restated as follows: let us drop the old methodologies, in order to be better able to see the new dimensions the technology is going to disclose to us. It is not time for calculation, but for a sort of deep contemplation of the everyday life surrounding the design and use of technology. Let truth be always our goal, but understood as the Greek word *Aletheia*: the unveiling of what lies hidden; this time what is concealed beneath the phenomena of work, organization, information, and technology.

3

Bricolage

The Internet, e-business, and e-commerce have shown many organizations the strategic role that ICTs can play in restructuring their internal processes and in establishing better and new links with suppliers, customers, and the public at large. On a closer look, however, the Internet has only reinforced and extended a trend in, so-called, strategic applications started in the late 1970s. Thirty years ago information systems may have been different in their infrastructure, network services, and applications portfolios. Still, pioneering companies like American Airlines, McKesson, and American Hospital Supply were already building the first strategic information systems (SIS)—interorganizational systems that linked internal MISs with customers, intermediaries, or suppliers and were able to create some form of competitive advantage. Based on these early successful SISs, methods were developed to design strategic ICT applications, which, with the diffusion of the

The chapter was originally published in a shorter version as C. U. Ciborra (1992), 'From thinking to tinkering: the grassroots of strategic information systems', *Information Society*, 8: 297–309.

Internet, would become the pillars of e-business and e-commerce. By reviewing those early efforts we can learn much about the origins, impacts, and limitations of the latest applications.

In general, the methods used to identify and develop strategic applications contain a few main prescriptions:

- a set of guidelines indicating how ICTs can support the business vis-à-vis the competition and an approach to planning and implementation;
- obtaining top management awareness;
- aligning the applications with the business strategy; and
- implementing applications that may generate competitive advantage.

It is ironic that in the early 1990s, even before the idea of B2B or B2C applications took the business world by storm, experienced practitioners and pioneers like M. D. Hopper, director of American Airlines' SABRE, were warning SIS enthusiasts that the old models that had proved successful in the earlier strategic applications of ICTs could hardly be applied any longer. The Internet brought about business models that were not, on closer inspection, that new.

There are valid economic and technical reasons indicating that Hopper's warning should be heeded in the Internet era.

Imitation has always been the driving force behind the diffusion of any technological innovation. SISs represent no exception. Unfortunately, if every major player in the industry adopts the same or similar applications, any competitive advantage evaporates. Systems that can be copied and built by a large number of firms, and where no firm enjoys any distinctive or sustainable advantage in implementation, can only generate normal economic returns. In particular, small firms are at a loss in applying standard SIS planning methods and solutions, for as price-takers they will find it very difficult to manipulate the industry structure to their advantage through the strategic use of ICTs.

Some interorganizational systems, as in the case of Electronic Data Interchange, require the connection of all the major firms in an industry: this undermines the competitive advantage that advocates claim such systems will offer to the individual firm.

More generally, market analysis of and the identification of SIS applications are research and consultancy services that can be purchased. They are carried out according to common frameworks, use standard data sources, and, if performed professionally, will reach similar results and recommend similar applications to similar firms.

It is not surprising, then, that before embarking on developing new applications, managers should ask themselves:

- does it really pay to be an innovator?
- are SISs offering true competitive advantage, or do they just represent a competitive necessity?
- how can a firm implement systems that cannot be copied easily, thus generating better than average returns over a reasonable period of time?

The more recent literature on strategic alignment has not challenged the generally held assumptions about business strategy formulation and industrial competition. Academics and practitioners following its tenets have been thwarted by the paradox of microeconomics: competition tends to force standardization of solutions, and equalization of production and coordination costs among participants. All these dynamics unfold *unless* a firm's strategy is imperfectly imitable: the more difficult it is for other firms to imitate a successful SIS, the longer a firm can obtain increased returns.

In order to escape from such a paradox, we argue that the construction of, or better the invention of, an SIS must be grounded on other foundations, both practically and conceptually.

To avoid easy imitation, the quest for a strategic application must be based on such intangible, and even opaque, areas as organizational culture. The investigation and enactment of unique sources of practice, know-how, and culture at firm and industry level can be the source of sustained advantage, rather than the structured analysis of internal assets and market structures.

Developing an SIS is much closer to prototyping and the deployment of end-user's ingenuity than has so far been appreciated: most strategic applications have emerged out of plain hacking. The capacity to integrate unique ideas and practical design solutions at the end-user level turns out to be more important than the adoption of structured approaches to systems development or industry analysis.

Such arguments cast a deep shadow on the current, widespread efforts firms are engaged in at the time of writing: the rush towards the application of ERP (Enterprise Resource Planning) packages creates similar business platforms for similar businesses. Again, the huge investments put into such systems lead to a new round of competitive necessity, but possibly little competitive advantage. However, it must be said that the level of successful implementation and standardization seems to be much lower than that promised by the software vendors and their allied consulting firms. Functioning ERP systems are still rare, so where they work they can be the source of a unique advantage. But this is not a chapter about the threats and promises of standardization (for that see the next chapter). It is a chapter about the celebration of hacking and *bricolage* in a strategic perspective.

Flimsy advantage

The rhetoric of SISs was based originally on an established and limited set of cases: both the early adopters, like McKesson, American Hospital Supply (then Baxter), and American Airlines; and those companies that went bankrupt in the 1980s because they did not adopt them, like Frontier Airlines and People Express. The plea in favour of SISs has been backed by frameworks for identifying strategic applications, like the value chain, or electronic integration and strategic alignment.

Less straightforward is the problem of how ICTs can provide a *sustainable* competitive advantage, in order that a pioneering company can extract a valuable performance edge from a strategic application. The widely cited SIS success stories often show that such systems provide only an ephemeral advantage, before being readily and rapidly copied by competitors.

Empirical studies showed very early on that, although the goals set by large corporations differ considerably (decreasing costs, electronic integration, differentiation, etc.), the driving force for the introduction of SISs is: either that other firms in the same industry have similar applications; or that systems are developed in collaboration with companies in the same industry; or that those genuinely innovative initiatives are soon copied by competitors. In sum, a large majority of applications and systems follow industry-wide trends: the very few really original ones will probably be promptly imitated.

These early studies concerned strategic systems developed ad hoc by large corporations. The diffusion of the Internet represents another powerful levelling factor. In the early days one could count on different technology platforms to deliver different performances; with the Internet this source of differentiation tends to vanish.

As a consequence, aiming at sustainable competitive advantage requires the continuous generation of innovative and competitive applications, and then the successful protection of the resulting quasi-rents over time. For example, some experts and consultants recommend that, in order to reap a long-term advantage from investments in distinctive SISs, a firm should carefully analyse the time it will take for competitors to develop a similar system; and it should look for asymmetries in organizational structure, culture, and size that may slow down competitors' successful deployment of the new applications.

Although such suggestions are valuable, they do not avoid the dilemmas inherent in SIS investment. If it is possible for the innovator to employ a consultancy firm to identify specific forces that can keep followers and imitators at bay, then the competitors can always hire consultants to strike back.

Evidently, then, more effective tactics for the development of strategic applications must challenge the approaches to *strategy formulation* and to *competition* that have pervaded the IS field since the 1980s. The critique of such approaches, together with a closer analysis of some of the exemplars, how they were conceived and built (or rather cultivated, see Chapter 5), indicates the central role of hacking and *bricolage* and suggests new tactics for identifying strategic applications. We will also need to look closer into the Internet itself to see how these old approaches increasingly fail to meet the needs of would-be innovators.

Alternative models of strategy and competition

Consider first the perspective on strategy formulation that has been imported from the business strategy literature into many SIS frameworks and methodologies. According to such a perspective, management should first engage in a strategy formulation process that is purely cognitive: key success factors and distinctive competencies are identified through the appraisal of the environment, its threats and opportunities, as well as the strengths and weaknesses of the organization; next, these factors and competencies are translated into a range of competitive strategy alternatives; then, once the optimal strategy has been selected and laid out in sufficient detail, the implementation phase follows.

This general, and seemingly obvious, approach holds to the tenets of rational management by keeping the phases of planning and implementation strictly separated. Specifically, as described by Mintzberg (1990), it is:

Conscious and analytic. Strategies emerge through a structured process of conscious thinking and rigorous analysis based on factual data. Implementation can take place only when the strategy has been formulated thoroughly. Strategic thinking aids are aimed at structuring any intuitive act and skill that is involved in the formulation phase.

Top-down and control oriented. Strategy is formulated at the peak of the managerial hierarchy. Responsibility for strategy rests with the chief executive officer: he or she formulates the strategic plan and then monitors its application throughout the various layers of the hierarchical control systems.

Simple and structured. Models of strategy formation must be made explicit and kept simple: data analysis and appraisal of internal and external intervening factors must be synthesized in clear, straightforward models (the value chain; the five forces; the diamond diagram; the BCG matrix; and their rivals).

Divided between action and structure. There is a separation between the process of thought that leads to a full-blown, articulated strategy and its subsequent implementation. Furthermore, the design of the organizational structure must follow the formulation and implementation processes.

Unfortunately, in everyday practice strategy formulation differs from such prescriptions and assumptions, as the following dilemmas point out. Incrementalism, muddling through, myopic and evolutionary decision making processes seem to prevail, even when there is a formal adherence to the principles listed above. Structures tend to influence the strategic formulations, before emerging as the result of the new vision, and the de facto involvement of actors other than the CEO is often manifested in the nature of the negotiation, and political, processes: conflicts and double binds set the stage where the strategy is conceived and formalized.

Mintzberg (1990) criticizes this school of strategic thinking on three main counts:

1. *Making strategy explicit?* The rational bias towards conscious thought and full, explicit articulation of strategy assumes, implicitly, that the environment is highly predictable and the unfolding of events is itself sequenced, so as to allow an orderly progression of formulation, design, and implementation. However, during implementation surprises often occur that call carefully developed plans into question. The need for continuous, opportunistic revisions clashes with the inflexibility of the formulation and implementation sequence.

Strict adherence to a rigid and explicit strategy formulation may hinder flexibility and adaptation to a changing environment, threatening the very attainment of the fit between the organization and the environment which represents the main purpose of the rationalist strategy approach.

2. *One-way relationship between strategy and structure?* In the conventional perspective, the strategist is regarded as an independent observer who can exercise judgement in a way that is removed from the everyday reality of the organization. For

example, when evaluating the strengths and weaknesses of the organization, or assessing the critical success factors, it is assumed that the strategist can think and make choices outside the influence of frames of reference, cultural biases, paralysing double binds, or ingrained, routinized ways of acting, behaving, and thinking. Although a considerable body of research shows that such biases are at work in any decision making process, they are assumed away by the quasi-scientific orientation of the rationalist approaches to strategy. Everyday life in businesses, on the other hand, shows that organizational structure, culture, inertia, and vicious circles influence the strategy formulation process, in addition to unexpected implementation outcomes. One can well conceive a strategy in an organizational vacuum and then mould the organization's structure accordingly, but this project will disregard the reciprocal ties between structure and the cognitive and behavioural processes of strategy formulation and planning.

3. *Thinking or learning?* Strategy formation tends to be seen as an intentional process of design, rather than as learning: the continuous acquisition of knowledge in various forms. We claim that strategy formulation is often likely to involve elements of surprise. There are sudden, radical shifts in the preferences, goals, and even identity of the decision makers, as well as paralysing vicious circles that may stifle the development and implementation of the strategy. Hence, strategic decision making must be based on effective adaptation and learning; both incremental, by trial and error, and radical, requiring second-order learning, where basic ways of looking at the environment and the organization's internal strengths and weaknesses can be continuously reassessed and reinvented.

Consider next the *models of competition* that are implicit in the SIS frameworks. Most of them rely on theories of business strategy derived from industrial economics. According to such a line of thought, returns to a firm are determined by the structure of the industry within which the firm operates. In order to achieve a competitive advantage a firm should manipulate the structural characteristics of the industry through ICT—by creating barriers to entry, product differentiation, links with suppliers, etc. However, there are alternative conceptions of competition that may be more relevant to SIS.

One contrasting alternative is the theory of monopolistic competition. In this view, firms are heterogeneous. They compete on the basis of certain resource and asset differences, such as those of technical know-how, reputation, ability to enact teamwork, organizational culture and skills, and other so-called 'invisible assets'. It is such differences that mean some firms are able to implement high return strategies. Competition then means cultivating unique strengths and capabilities, and defending such uniqueness against imitation by other firms.

Another perspective on competition sees it as a process of innovation in products, markets, organization, and technology. Innovation is here more the outcome of the capitalist process of 'creative destruction' (Schumpeter 1950) than the result of a strategic planning process. Ability at guessing, learning, and sheer luck appear to be the key competitive factors in such a perspective.

At this point we can contrast two alternative packages, containing different sets of ideas about business strategy and competition, that are relevant to designing a strategic application. According to the first, strategy gets formulated before the fact, is based on careful industry analysis, and consists of a series of moves that can be planned and implemented to gain advantage through the manipulation of the industry structure. According to the second, strategy formulation is difficult to plan before the event, and competitive advantage stems from the exploitation of unique, intangible characteristics of the firm (including its networks of relations) and the unleashing of its innovative capabilities. The comparison between the two SIS packages is not merely an academic exercise.

A closer look at some SIS applications will disclose a wide gap between the prevailing declared methodologies, closer to the first package, and successful business and ICT innovations, definitely closer to the latter.

True stories

It is now appropriate, after so much conceptual discussion, to turn to the empirical evidence. Specifically, one can ask whether systems and applications that have proved over the years to be of strategic importance for the organizations and communities that have adopted them have emerged out of careful planning and structured methods or from less linear, more happenstance, developments. To provide an answer to this legitimate question, we consider various examples: ranging from famous early SIS applications in individual organizations to systems and networks whose strategic impact has changed for ever the role of computers in society.

The first set of cases comprises the SIS classics: Baxter's ASAP, McKesson's Economost, and American Airlines' SABRE. In the second group we find the French Videotex Teletel (better known by the name of the PTT terminals, Minitel) and the *mother* of all networks, the Internet. At a closer look, all these cases emphasize the discrepancy between, on the one hand, ideal methodologies and plans and, on the other, the realities of implementation, where chance, serendipity, trial and error, or even gross negligence seem to play a major role in shaping systems that will become of strategic importance and reference, but only after the fact.

ASAP, the system launched by AHS Corporation (subsequently acquired by Baxter), started as an operational, localized response to a customer need. Because of difficulties in serving a hospital effectively, a manager of a local AHS office had the idea of giving pre-punched cards to the hospital's purchasing department; the ordering clerks could then transfer the content of the cards expeditiously through a phone terminal. From this local ad-hoc solution to a particular problem, the idea gradually emerged of linking all the customer hospitals in the same way through touch-tone telephones, bar code readers, teletypes, and eventually PCs. At a later stage AHS management realized the positive impact such an electronic link with the customers could have on profits and were able to allocate adequate resources for its further development.

McKesson's Economost, another pioneering order entry system, started in a similar way. The former IS manager later admitted that 'behind the legend' there was simply a local initiative by one of the business units. The system was not developed according to a company-wide strategic plan; rather, it was the outcome of an evolutionary, piecemeal process that included the ingenious tactical use of systems already available. Economost was stumbled upon almost accidentally, the outcome of what the French call *bricolage*—tinkering that may lead to a serendipitous outcome.

SABRE, the first computerized reservation system built by American Airlines in the 1970s, was, likewise, not originally conceived as a biased distribution channel in order to create entry barriers to competitors, while tying in travel agents. It began as a relatively straightforward, ad-hoc inventory database addressing a specific need that had nothing to do with ensuring a competitive advantage. On the contrary, it was supposed to solve an internal inefficiency: American's relative inability, compared to other airlines, to monitor the inventory of available seats and to link passenger names with booked seats in a more reliable way.

Another telling case, this time at national level, is represented by Minitel, the only successful public Videotex system, which gave the French, in the mid-1990s, an edge on e-commerce that lasted up to the end of the decade. Thanks to its six million terminals, and an average of eighteen calls a month per owner, the system generated a volume of transactions (mostly confined to France) which rivalled the beginnings of Internet commercial traffic worldwide.

The initial concept of Minitel was not very innovative. It scaled the model of a centralized MIS up to a national level. Mainframes allowed the creation of large centralized databases providing information that could be sold and accessed by a large number of customers using dumb terminals. Such Videotex systems failed both for early adopters, like the UK Post Office, and for latecomers, like the German Bundespost, even though they could benefit from better technology, more careful planning, and the experience of others. France Telecom (formerly, Direction Générale des Télécommunications, DGT) moved into Videotex relatively late. However, there were significant differences in the way the system was promoted to the general public. The strategic vision of the *informatisation de la société* convinced the government to make Minitel a success through the diffusion of millions of free terminals. The free distribution is seen by observers and competitors as French Videotex's main success factor. This is only half of the truth: the free terminals were at the time a necessary condition for success, as the launch occurred before mass ownership of personal computers, but not a sufficient one. Nonetheless, at the beginning the use of Minitel was sluggish, probably for the same reason other Videotex systems never took off: people had other habitual ways of seeking the information contained in the centralized databases.

The network also had other applications; for example it was a public e-mail service, but the DGT never promoted it as such. This facility was only discovered and used by millions of users nationwide because an act of hacking attracted the interest of the national press. During an experiment in Strasbourg, when a local newspaper put its classified ads section on Videotex, a hacker—probably located at the data processing centre of the newspaper itself—started using the Minitel to respond to the ads, establishing a direct, electronic dialogue with their authors. This was the beginning of the perception and use of Minitel as an electronic mail system (*messagerie*), rather than just as a dumb terminal able to access large databases. At that point the number of terminals in homes turned out to represent the critical mass that could start a virtuous circle: for one thing, it created a new marketplace where many independent business providers could sell their services. People immediately used the 'new' medium so much that the national backbone packet switched network, Transpac, broke down due to the overload. France Telecom was flexible and pragmatic enough to adapt the infrastructure technically and commercially to the new pattern of usage that had emerged outside its initial vision and plans, 'moving from the logic of storage to the logic of traffic'.

The early days of the Internet, and its predecessor ARPANET, are also full of *bricolage*, hacking, improvisations, and serendipity. ARPANET was not funded and built to be a medium for interpersonal communication; it was intended to allow scientists to share computer resources at a distance. It was about networked time-sharing systems; not about e-mail. In the early 1970s, driven by that vision, ARPANET did not take off as expected and it was far from being an undisputed success. What helped to transform a research network into the full-blown Internet was a myriad of hacks, surprises, and improvisations, mostly stemming from the users' environment, and the benevolent and tolerant ARPA project management practices. Again, electronic mail was the innovation that made the network take off. The new service was not the result of planning but of a 'nice hack': an inspired piece of programming developed by a local user to exchange messages between minicomputers at a host site. Another good hack was to piggyback the new program onto the ARPANET file-transfer protocol, which happened to be being defined at that time. Situated add-ons and serendipitous piggybacking substitute for absent plans and visions, absent because very few specialists were then paying attention to electronic messaging. By 1973 three-quarters of all the traffic on ARPANET was e-mail. As a result the late 1970s completion reports of the ARPANET research program note that the largest single surprise of the whole program was the unplanned and unanticipated success of electronic mail. A local user hack had big consequences: almost immediately it caused a radical shift in the identity of ARPANET. It multiplied in turn the scope and impact of the process that originated it in the first place: e-mail dramatically extended the user community, out of this enlarged community even more hacks and surprises would originate. For example, the World Wide Web was conceived in another user organization, CERN in Geneva, where a specialist, drawing from the hacker counter-culture, extended the notion of hypertext to an inter-network scale. Again his goal was limited and aimed at addressing a local need: accessing and organizing multimedia documents over many networked sites to support the collaborative style of research work in the particle physics laboratory.

All these cases recount the same tale: innovative, strategic applications of ICT are not fully designed top-down or introduced in one shot; rather they are tried out through prototyping and tinkering. In contrast, strategy formulation and design take place within pre-existing cognitive frames and institutional contexts that usually prevent designers and sponsors from seeing and exploiting the potential for innovation hidden in the artefacts.

We encounter a paradox. In order to achieve a new SIS design the issue is neither to try to generate the most creative application idea, nor to realize the design through a careful planning and implementation method. The real issue is being able to overcome those cognitive and institutional barriers that prevent users and designers seeing, appreciating, and utilizing all those potential applications *already* surrounding the members of an organization.

On the other hand, precisely because of such barriers, no method or planning exercise, nor any brainstorming and vision generating exercise, can enable managers and designers to specify completely an SIS *ex ante*. Design, implementation, and use consistently show unexpected consequences: events, behaviours, and features of systems and people who use them that fall outside the scope of the original specifications. SISs emerge when early adopters are able to recognize, in use, some idiosyncratic features that were ignored, devalued, or simply unplanned.

Searching for new strategic systems

The preceding discussion on the models of competition has pointed out that if the SIS application does not generate value, it may not be worth developing. If it is not rare, it may just be a competitive necessity in order to obtain normal, not superior, returns. If it is easily imitable, it can only deliver a short-term, contestable advantage.

The question is, then, how to achieve rarity and imperfect imitability in designing an SIS, if models of strategic thinking and competitive environment proposed from the 1980s onward do not work?

The cases consistently indicate that the development of applications that can deliver a sustained competitive advantage must be treated as an innovation process. To innovate means to create new knowledge about resources, goals, tasks, markets, products, and processes. The skills and competencies available in the corporation represent at the same time the source of, and the constraint for, innovation.

There are two alternative routes for the creation of new knowledge. The first is to rely on local information and stick to routine behaviour and extend it gradually to cope with a new task: learning by doing; incremental decision making; muddling through. When an adequate level of competence is not available in relation to the complexity of the vision and project at hand, accessing more diverse and distant information and engaging in far-off experimentation would cause errors and divergence from optimal performance.

This approach requires allowing and even encouraging tinkering by people close to the operational level, combining and applying known tools and routines to solve new problems. No general scheme or model is available: only local cues from a situation are trusted and exploited in a somewhat blind and unreflective way. The aim is to achieve ad-hoc solutions by applying heuristics rather than high theory. Systems like ASAP or the Minitel were developed in this way: even when big plans were present, it was *bricolage* and hacking that led to the innovation. The value of tinkering lies in keeping the development of an SIS close to the competencies of the organization and its continual adaptations of local practices.

The second route to innovation is to attack the competency gap at its roots, allowing new competencies to emerge and replace the existing ones. This is a process of radical learning that entails restructuring the cognitive and organizational contexts that endow the practices, routines, and skills at hand with meaning. This approach leads to new systems and arrangements; not by random walks or tinkering, on the contrary it intentionally challenges, and smashes, established routines, frames, and institutional arrangements. In particular it attacks those that govern competency acquisition, learning-by-doing, and learning by trial and error.

From this point of view, designing an innovative SIS would involve more than market study, systems analysis, requirements specifications, and interest accommodation. Rather, it deals primarily with the structures and frames within which such exercises take place: with shaping and restructuring the context of both business policy and systems development. Such a formative context can be made explicit and changed only by intervening in situations and by designing-in-action.

Once the background context is restructured-in-action, participants are freer to devise new strategies, and to look at the environment and the organizational capabilities in radically new ways. New strategic information and information systems will be generated, based on the unique, emerging world view the designers and users are able to adopt. As a result, we can expect organizations and SIS to be very different from standard solutions and difficult to imitate, for they imply that competitors must abandon not only their old practices and conceptions, but also the contexts in which they routinely solve problems, run systems, and build new ones.

Both routes to SIS touch those grey areas of work practices, beliefs, moods, values, routines, and cultures which lie at the core of organizing. Along the incremental route these provide the background conditions, the cultural bed for tinkering: new systems and applications emerge from the enactment and reinforcement of local innovations. Along the radical route, a newly acquired awareness of the formative context, the prevailing frames and institutional arrangements, and the ability to revise that context radically paves the way for novel systems and business models.

The virtues of *bricolage*

In order to understand *bricolage*, first we must go below the surface of the practice of *bricolage* and other kindred activities, such as serendipity, hacking, and improvisation. (This is also considered in Chapter 8.)

As soon we leave the realm of method, procedure, and systematic ways of organizing and executing work according to rational study, planning, and control we enter the murky world of informal, worldly, and everyday modes of operation and practices. It is the realm of hacking; practical intelligence; the artistic embroidery of the prescribed procedure; the short cut and the transgression of the established organizational order as embedded in systems and formalized routines. *Bricolage*, improvisation, and hacking are terms that are often used, in various domains of activity, to describe such modes of operation. They differ slightly in meaning, but they have many aspects in common and the latter are perhaps the most important. Since they diverge from the formalized, pre-planned ways of operating, their outcomes may well lead to serendipity, to the possibility of finding something valuable that was not sought for at the outset (this recalls many of the key technical choices made during the development of the Internet).

Another characteristic of these modes of operating is that they have an uncertain status, always at the boundary between highly competent behaviour and incompetence. Calling someone a *bricoleur* or an improviser can, in some contexts and cultures, be an insult equivalent to labelling someone as unprofessional, and hacking in some contexts is talked about as a crime. These derogatory perceptions testify that these activities are sanctioned as marginal, belonging to the red light districts of the organization. Being at the margins of the formalized procedures grants improvisers an added element of liberty, and sometimes of play, about the choices of which resources to harness and how. If these approaches look rough compared to neat and tidy formal procedures, they are on the other hand highly situated: they tend to include an added element of ingenuity, experience, and skill belonging to the individual and their community (of practice) rather than to the organizational systems. Finally, they all seem to share the same way of operating: small forces, tiny interventions, and on-the-fly add-ons lead, when performed skilfully and with close attention to the local context, to momentous consequences, unrelated to the speed and scope of the initial intervention. These modes of operation unfold in a dance that always includes the key aspects of localness and time (the 'here and now'); modest intervention and large-scale effects; on-the-fly appearance but deeply rooted in personal and collective skill and experience.

There are then slightly different nuances on each term. *Bricolage* (from the late Latin *bricola* catapult) means tinkering through the combination of resources at hand. These resources become the tools and they define *in situ* the heuristic to solve the problem. 'Let the world help you': *bricolage* is about leveraging the world as defined by the situation. With *bricolage*, the practices and the situations disclose new uses and applications of the technology and the things.

Improvisation (see Chapter 8) puts an emphasis on the suddenness, extemporaneity, and unpredictability of the human intervention, though highly situated. Competent improvisation involves a registering of, and intervention in, the situation that seems for the outside observer almost out of context, since it is fast and unexpected. Improvisation thus adds a reference to the speed of the mode of operation, and to (ex)temporality in general.

The dictionary defines hacking as 'cutting with irregular or unskilful blows'. In the jargon of computer practice, hacking is devising and implementing a program to perform a certain useful function, by making use of any technology in an original, unorthodox, and often playful way. Such a program is not isolated but fits into a larger application environment. Still, it is a hack because technology is used in a way that it is not supposed to be. Hacking stands to software engineering tenets as *bricolage* stands to organizational procedures. Thus, while software development should take place according to orderly sequences of activities (specifications; analysis; design; implementation; debugging; usability testing; etc.), hacking is an ingenious activity that through iterations, reuse, and reinterpretations of the existing programming environment leads to the implementation of new solutions. Experts underline the fact that hacking has been proved to succeed (as in the case of the creation of the Linux operating system). It transcends the orthodox, centralized, and staged view of software development by replacing it with a distributed and evolutionary approach. Because of the nature of most large-scale software production tasks, hacking, though undertaken individually (the hacker-nerd), tends to take place in a community (of hackers), where the rigid boundaries indicated by software engineering, such as analyst, user, application programmer, or debugger, fall apart. The participants in the hacker community are able to play all these roles interchangeably according to the circumstances of the project.

The power of *bricolage*, improvisation, and hacking is that these activities are highly situated; they exploit, in full, the local context and resources at hand, while often pre-planned ways of operating appear to be derooted, and less effective because they do not fit the contingencies of the moment. Also, almost by definition, these activities are highly idiosyncratic, and tend to be invisible both because they are marginalized and because they unfold in a way that is small in scope. The results are modes of operating that are latent and not easy to imitate. Thus, the smart *bricolage* or the good hack cannot be easily replicated outside the cultural bed from which it has emerged.

Planning by oxymorons

The radical learning route to generating continuously innovative SIS designs, fighting the paradox of microeconomics due to imitation, consists in proceeding by moves that appear to the current managerial wisdom as oxymorons. Along this route, gaining new knowledge does not entail following a procedure, attending to a methodology, and actuating a plan, but fusing opposites in practice, and exposing oneself to the anomalies that are bound to occur. Consider then the following oxymorons as alternative guidelines, capable of augmenting the organization's skills in developing an SIS. The first four oxymorons are aimed at transforming *bricolage* and learning-by-doing into activities that increase the probability of stumbling upon new strategic applications. Their potential stems from a simple idea for most organizations: emerging, spontaneous mission-oriented operations (collective hacking efforts, for example) need to be recognized and given room to move. The remaining three oxymorons set specific conditions for radical learning and innovation.

To bolster incremental learning:

1. *Value bricolage strategically.* The more volatile the markets and the technology, the more likely it is that effective solutions need to be embedded in everyday experience and local knowledge, since change triggers adaptation and adjustment. This is the Petri dish for tinkering and hacking; here creative applications that have strategic impact are invented, engineered, and tried out.

2. *Design tinkering.* Activities, settings, and systems have to be arranged so that prototyping by end-users can flourish, together with open experimentation. It requires the setting up of organizational arrangements that favour local innovation, like intrapreneurship or ad-hoc project teams. Ethnographic studies of systems and practices, and design processes that are linked to the local idiosyncrasies of actors, settings, and circumstances, can represent designed activities aimed at discovering emerging, or natural, experiments and innovations.

3. *Establish systematic serendipity.* In open experimentation, designs are largely incomplete, while implementation and refinement intermingle constantly. Conception and execution tend to be concurrent: simultaneous rather than sequential. This is the ideal context for serendipity to emerge and lead to unexpected solutions.

4. *Thrive on gradual breakthroughs*. In a fluctuating environment, ideas and solutions are bound to emerge that do not square with established organizational routines: deviations, incongruencies, and mismatches will populate the design and development agenda. This is the raw material for innovation, and managers should appreciate and learn about such emerging practices, giving up any wish to control and restore the previous routines.

To establish the preconditions for radical learning and innovation:

5. *Practise unskilled learning*. If incremental learning takes place within cognitive and organizational arrangements and does not challenge them, it is condemned to provide solutions that are not innovative—the so-called learning trap. The cognitive and organizational structures that support learning can be challenged in action, but this may lead to incompetent behaviour—mistakes, as assessed in relation to the old routines. Managers should value such behaviour as an attempt to unlearn the old ways of thinking and doing that may lead to new perspectives from which to look at resources, actions, and systems.

6. *Strive for failure*. Usually, striving for excellence suggests trying to do better what it is already known how to do, or imitating what others are already doing, for example through benchmarking. Such behaviours pave the way to routinized, though efficient, systems and procedures—the competency trap. Creative reflection over failures, rather than rigid control aimed at uncertainty reduction, can indicate the road to novel ideas, designs, and implementations, and the recognition of discontinuities and flex points.

7. *Achieve collaborative inimitability*. In order to enhance uniqueness and imperfect imitability do not be afraid to collaborate, even with competitors, in developing strategic applications: expose the

organization to new cultures and ideas, to improve the skills of learning by intrusion, and to find clues for new, significant changes in the most obvious routines of another organization.

These oxymorons represent a systematic approach for the establishment of an organizational environment where new knowledge, and thus new systems, can be generated. Precisely because they are paradoxical, they can unfreeze existing routines, cognitive frames, and behaviours. They favour learning over monitoring, innovation over control.

To conclude, behind the effective and sustainable enactment of strategic applications of ICT there are mundane modes of operation, such as *bricolage*, improvisation, or hacking. The bubbling up of new ideas from the bottom of the organization can lead to acts of incremental or radical innovation, whereby the existing organizational reality, the environment, and ICT applications are seen anew by the members. In the latter case SISs are intimately associated with business renewal.

With the modern, ubiquitous information infrastructures (think of the diffusing ERP packages and the Internet) firms build similar platforms and access the same data. Competitive advantage related to ICTs can only stem from the cognitive and organizational capability to convert such systems, applications, and data into practical, situated, and unique knowledge for action.

SIS applications are those that are developed close to and serve the grass roots of the organization, where its core competencies and skills are daily deployed and perfected thanks to the myriad invisible acts of *bricolage* and hacking. Managers and specialists need to appreciate local fluctuations in systems practices as the repository of unique innovations and commit adequate resources and attention to their cultivation, even if, or especially when, they fly in the face of more established, structured approaches.

4

Gestell

Since the second half of the 1990s IBM has been leading the way in formulating and deploying an extensive new fabric of processes and tools in order to be able to operate efficiently as a truly global company. One such global business process has been Customer Relationship Management (CRM).

CRM consists of an array of processes that streamline all the activities between IBM and its customers across markets, product lines, and locations. It involves more than 100,000 employees worldwide and is based on a variety of existing and new systems and applications that automate and link multiple business processes. The logic of CRM is quite straightforward despite the myriad activities involved and the many people it affects. It is supposed to be the backbone of the successful completion of any business transaction IBM is engaged in: from the initial identification of opportunities through to order fulfilment and customer satisfaction evaluation. Thus, CRM prescribes what is

The chapter was originally published as C. U. Ciborra and O. Hanseth (1998), 'From tool to Gestell', *Information Technology and People* 11/4: 305–27.

needed to execute a full negotiation cycle around any customer transaction (the ideas and models developed by Winograd and Flores (1987) were explicitly considered by the internal IBM team when it developed the new processes). The complex bundle of processes, roles, and IT tools that form the main components of CRM can be viewed as part of the corporate infrastructure of the new, global firm. Internally, CRM has been nicknamed the 'new plumbing of IBM'.

A corporate infrastructure is shared by a vast number of users in various departments across the entire organization; a variety of standard ways of operating are embedded in procedures, software, and hardware; it requires the standardization of many existing practices and systems; it links applications and people according to a defined sequence of business purposes. Finally, it is deployed and maintained through a set of management and consulting units and practices.

Cases like CRM represent a good empirical point of departure for a journey around the role played by ICT as corporate information infrastructure. Our journey starts from considering the management agenda that governs the deployment of such technologies (what one may call the 'appearances' of infrastructure management models and prescriptions). Next, we need to investigate what is taken for granted or relegated to the margins of such an agenda—what we might call surprising or unexpected 'apparitions'. The management agenda is based on a set of assumptions and various forms of obviousness that often obscure, rather than clarify, what is at stake in the governance of complex infrastructures. Thus, the apparitions are a sign that such hidden assumptions clash with the actual implementation of the new infrastructure (see the Methodological Appendix).

We need, then, to move beyond the management agenda to try to make sense of the apparitions. We will do this by referring to the economic study of infrastructures. This study will point to some key limitations of the conventional management approaches. For example, economists suggest that what may appear to managers and consultants as an aberration or a limiting case is, in reality, a much commoner occurrence: infrastructure as an installed base is more often than not 'out of control', and tactics to govern it are much more subtle and limited than the impression one gets when following management methods and models. Furthermore, the study of recalcitrance and wide-range effects of infrastructure, if not its autonomy, carried out through the lens of actor network theory (Latour 1999) can further enlarge and evolve our perspective. Finally, tapping Heidegger's questioning about the essence of technology, we will explore an intriguing insight which is able to evoke a new disposition and understanding ('management' will appear by then too strong a word) of the technology itself.

Alignment and control

Corporate infrastructure as a concept emerged within the management literature of the 1980s in relation to the planning of company-wide information systems. Initially, emphasis was placed on the standardization of systems and data throughout the corporation, as a way of reconciling the centralized IS department and resources on the one hand, and the distribution of systems and applications on the other. More recent developments in network technologies have drawn attention to the data and document communication aspect of infrastructure.

Schematically, the management (and consulting) agenda, concerning the creation and governance of corporate infrastructures, follows this sequence of activities:

- Analysis of the firm's strategic context so as to elicit the key business drivers.

- A joint consideration of the need to improve or transform existing business processes and infrastructure. Formulation and implementation of relevant BPR and technical change plans.
- Envisioning the related changes in roles, responsibilities, incentives, skills, and organizational structures required by BPR and infrastructure reforms.

According to this agenda, managing an infrastructure requires dealing with problems such as: aligning strategy with ICT architecture, key business processes, and information requirements; ubiquitous access and use of ICT resources; standardization; interoperability of systems and applications through protocols and gateways; flexibility, resilience, and security. The infrastructure must reconcile local variety and proliferation of applications with centralized planning and control over systems and business processes.

Defining the value of variables such as reach and scope sets the boundaries and contents of the infrastructure. Reach refers to the number of activities or processes actually touched by the infrastructure, while scope refers to the type and variety of applications that it supports (the range of processes being partially or totally automated through the infrastructure). Depending upon these two variables, and especially the strategic intent of the firm, the infrastructure can play different roles, from being a utility or a fully-fledged SIS.

Empirical studies about, and reflection upon, the management of infrastructures point out some problematic aspects of the straightforward management agenda. For example, is it better to have a highly flexible infrastructure that enables the firm to seize a wide range of future, unplanned business redesign options, or an infrastructure that is perfectly aligned with the current strategic intent? Thus, should one aim for alignment, as repeatedly suggested by the management literature, or for flexibility? Extensive reviews of top managers' opinions seem to lead to no clear-cut conclusions.

To be sure, the agendas that spell out what to do in order to extract the maximum capability from corporate infrastructures include some telling caveats, such as:

- aligning business and technology strategies is an ongoing executive responsibility: 'strategic alignment is a journey, not an event';
- managers must be ready to learn and adapt, no matter what the alignment pattern selected at one point in time;
- there are expression barriers that prevent the clear articulation of the strategic intent of the firm, and thus hamper the effort for an explicit strategic alignment;
- there are barriers that due to political, cultural, or economic factors impede the smooth implementation of any strategic plan concerning infrastructure.

The caveats seem to restate the same message: the world out there is complicated and cannot be captured fully by a static model, because of the unavoidable difference between models and real life.

However, these almost obvious caveats render the management agenda largely irrelevant to action, since it fails to address the central issue of *implementation*: the key transition between the conception of a vision and the realization of that vision. Management agendas look and sound practical but they are deceivingly persuasive. They cannot be translated into effective actions, being highly simplified and based on sweeping generalizations and abstractions (such as 'strategy', 'utility', and 'infrastructure'). The remainder of this chapter is dedicated to getting closer to the 'of course', the obvious dismissal of the intricacies of 'real life' that 'naturally' cannot be captured by a model (the apparitions), and to human experience, to which the caveats implicitly make reference. This represents at the same time the Achilles' heel of the management models and the point to access alternative vistas.

The tactics of cultivation

The management agenda is not only deceptively sound, simple, and highly abstract; it is also too narrow. It restricts our view of infrastructure to seeing only a large MIS, in which systems and applications may be heterogeneous, but control and resource allocation can be, and ought to be, centralized. However, the case of large, national infrastructures reminds us that their management transcends the boundaries of centralized, hierarchical control of a resource. Economics, and especially the economics of standards and network infrastructures, can help us in overcoming the narrow MIS mindset that lurks within many managerial discourses on infrastructure.

One could start the economic analysis by looking at the problem of pricing; that is, how to price the service given by a common, collective good. The notion of pricing a public good has several facets: how to let people who use more, pay more; how to avoid free riding; what is the trade-off between delivery of a universal service and a customized service; how to reach a *critical mass* of users? But also, who should pay for the positive and/or negative *externalities* generated by use? How to cope with the issues of installed base (infrastructure inertia) and flexibility (the costs of infrastructure change)?

Beyond their economic relevance, correct and balanced answers to such questions form key factors influencing the take-off and long-term growth of any infrastructure. They also point to a more general issue: the scope for control over an infrastructure is always limited, and management have to live with a resource that they can only incompletely harness. Correspondingly, the governance of infrastructure is a problem, not a given, since there can be multiple stakeholders with conflicting interests. In sum, the infrastructure can expand and grow in directions and to an extent that is largely outside the control of any individual stakeholder.

Building large infrastructures takes time: all elements are connected. As time passes, new requirements appear which the infrastructure has to adapt to. A whole infrastructure cannot be changed instantly—the new has to be integrated with the old. The new version must be designed so as to be compatible with the old, existing infrastructure, in order to facilitate 'interoperability' between the two. Hence, the old—the installed base—heavily influences how the new can be designed: infrastructures can only be developed through extending and improving the *installed base*.

The latter notion suggests that infrastructures are considered as always already existing; they are *never* developed from scratch. When a 'new' infrastructure is designed, it must always be integrated into and thus be an extension of others, or it will replace one component of another, larger, infrastructure. This has been the case in the building of all transport infrastructures: every single road—even the first one, if it makes sense to speak about such a thing—has been built in this way; when air traffic infrastructures have been created, they have been tightly interwoven with, and dependent on, road and railway networks—these other infrastructures were needed for travel between airports and the final destination. A large information infrastructure is not just hard to change. It might also be a powerful actor influencing its own future life—its extension and size as well as its form.

Next, the issue of standards can be considered as part of a more general phenomenon labelled 'self-reinforcing mechanisms' and 'network externalities'. Self-reinforcing mechanisms emerge when the value of a particular product or technology for individual adopters increases as the number of adopters grows. A standard which builds up an installed base ahead of its competitors becomes cumulatively more attractive, making the choice of standards path dependent and highly influenced by small benefits demonstrated in the early stages.

Information infrastructures are paradigmatic examples of phenomena where network externalities and positive feedback (increasing return on increasing adoption) are crucial, and accordingly technologies are easily locked in and made irreversible. The positive feedback from new users is strong. The utility of an infrastructure technology is not only dependent on the number of users; in the case of e-mail, for instance, it also coincides to a large extent with its number of users. Technology becomes hard to modify as successful changes need to be compatible with the installed base (so-called path dependency). As the number of users grows, reaching agreement about new features as well as coordinating transitions becomes increasingly difficult. Vendors develop products incorporating a standard and new technologies are built on top of it. As the installed base grows, institutions like standardization bodies are established and the interests vested in the technology expand. It follows that designing and governing an infrastructure differs from designing an MIS, due to the far-reaching influence of the installed base and the self-reinforcing mechanisms, including lock-ins and path dependency.

An infrastructure is not just a complex, shared tool that management are free to align according to their strategy. In this respect the economic perspective highlights a much more limited and opportunistic agenda involving trade-offs, dilemmas, and a number of constraints, such as:

- *Narrow policy windows.* There may be only brief and uncertain time windows during which effective interventions can be made at moderate resource costs.
- *Blind giants.* Decision makers are likely to have the greatest power to influence the future trajectories of network technologies just when a suitable knowledge basis on which to make system-wide optimal choices among alternatives is most lacking. These actors, then, resemble blind giants— one would wish to improve their vision before their power dissipates.
- *Angry orphans.* Some groups of users will be left orphaned; they will have sunk investments in systems and standards whose maintenance and further development are going to be discontinued.

One can imagine differing governance tactics, such as that of counter-action—to prevent the policy window from slamming shut before the policy makers are able to perceive the shape of their relevant future options more clearly. This requires positive action to maintain leverage over systems rivalry, preventing any of the currently available variants from becoming too deeply entrenched as a standard, and so gathering more information about technological opportunities even at the cost of immediate losses in operational efficiency. Possibly, the most important remedy to help overcome the effects of positive feedback and network externalities, lock-in, and inefficiency is the construction of gateways and adapters. Gateways may connect heterogeneous networks which are being built independently or based on different versions of the same standards. Typically, building *gateway devices* linking otherwise incompatible systems can help to minimize the static economic losses incurred by orphans.

Relying on these and other tactics can fundamentally change the scope of the management agenda. Whilst from a technical and strictly managerial perspective the purpose is to design, build, align, and control an infrastructure, the economic perspective suggests that cultivating an installed base is a wiser and sounder strategy. The concept of cultivation focuses on the limits of rational, human control. Technological systems could be regarded as 'organisms with a life of their own' and cultivating would mean developing tactics of interaction with such an organism. Cultivation accepts the idea of the power of natural systems to withstand our effort at design, either by disarming them or by ruining them by breakdown.

The actor network perspective

Considering technological systems as 'organisms with a life of their own' implies, at the extreme, that one can look at technology itself as an *actor*. Infrastructures are then socio-technical networks where components, usually considered as social or technological, are linked together into networks (Latour 1999). The development organization as well as the product being developed is considered as a set of complex socio-technical networks. Acknowledging the importance of the installed base implies that our traditional notions of design, as performed by humans only, have to be rejected. The idea of cultivation as the outcome of development carried out by multiple agents (one of which can be the installed base or the infrastructure standards) captures quite effectively the interactive role of both humans and technology. The installed base is a powerful actor; its future cannot be consciously designed, but developers do have influence—they might cultivate it. The installed base acts in two ways: it can be regarded as an actor involved in each single development activity; but, perhaps more importantly, it plays a crucial role as a mediator and coordinator between the independent, non-technological actors and the development activities. If humans strive for control, making the world appropriate for engineering tasks, strategies for cultivating infrastructures can be considered strategies for fighting against the power of the installed base.

To enrich the management agenda applying this line of reasoning we can tap various streams of research stemming from the field of the social studies of science and technology. Specifically, the actor network perspective looks at technological, human, and social elements as tied together into networks, based on the assumption that technologies are always defined as working in an environment that includes non-technological elements—without which the technology would be meaningless and, further, would not work. In the same way, humans use non-human objects (technologies and other artefacts) in all their dealings—our life and the roles we play in the world are based upon the existence of these very objects. Neither humans nor technological artefacts should be considered as pure, isolated elements, but as heterogeneous networks. Elements in such a network are not initially defined as human, social, or technological; they are referred to by a new term—*actant*. These assumptions do not deny any differences, or borders, between what is social or human and what is technological. However, these borders are seen as negotiated, not as given.

Two concepts from the actor network perspective are of particular relevance for enlarging the infrastructure agenda: *inscription* and *translation*.

The notion of inscription refers to the way technical artefacts embody patterns of use. During the design process, the developer works out a scenario for how the infrastructure will be used. This scenario is inscribed into the infrastructure. The inscription includes *programmes of action* for the users, and defines roles to be played by users and the infrastructure. By inscribing programmes of action into a piece of technology, for example through ERP applications, technology becomes an actant imposing its inscribed programme of action onto its users. To have any effect, programmes of action should not only be inscribed into isolated technological components, but rather into aligned networks of technologies, humans, and social institutions.

The inscription of patterns of use may not succeed because the actual use deviates from it. Rather than following the assigned programme of action, a user may use the system in an unanticipated way; she may follow an anti-programme. When studying the use of technical artefacts one necessarily shifts back and forth between the designer's projected user and the real user in order to describe this dynamically negotiated process of design (see Chapter 5).

The strength of inscriptions, whether they must be followed or can be avoided, depends on the *irreversibility* of the actor network they are inscribed into. It is never possible to know beforehand, but by studying the sequence of attempted inscriptions one can learn more about exactly how, and by means of which inscriptions, a given aim is achieved.

A different style of managing alignment emerges at this point. Stability and social order, according to the actor network perspective, are continually negotiated as a social process of aligning interests. As actors from the outset have a diverse set of interests, stability rests crucially on the ability to *translate*, that is, reinterpret, represent, or appropriate, others' interests to one's own.

Design is translation—the interests of users and others may, according to typical ideal models, be translated into specific needs, the specific needs are further translated into more general and unified ones, so that these may be translated eventually into one and the same solution.

Finally, just as economics does, the social studies of technology indicate that a key feature of infrastructures is the difficulty of changing them as they gain momentum. The concept of the (possible) irreversibility of an aligned network captures the accumulated resistance against change quite nicely. It describes how translations between actor networks are made durable, and how they can resist assaults from competing translations. The degree of irreversibility depends both on the extent to which it is subsequently impossible to go back to a point where that translation was only one amongst others; and also on the extent to which it shapes and determines subsequent translations.

Perhaps the crucial issue in the design and take-off of infrastructures is the settlement of standards. Traditionally, standards are considered as both universal and purely technical in the sense that there is one superior definition satisfying the systems requirements and the needs of all users. Once defined, they are able to ensure that all correct local implementations will work uniformly and consistently.

This view is not supported by the findings of science and technology studies. What has been repeatedly discovered by studying laboratories where scientific facts are ascertained and established is the local and situated nature of all scientific and technical knowledge. Scientific results are obtained within specific local contexts, but context is then deleted and the results reconstructed as universal. In the same way, infrastructure standards are far from being pure technical artefacts. They should be looked at, rather, as complex, heterogeneous actor networks.

Further, standards are shaped by their history and context of origin. They are not objectively reflecting some reality or neutral technical solutions and tools. They embed social and political elements. If the management agenda, driven by a science bias, aims at building infrastructure by defining universal standards, the social studies of technology perspective urges us not to disregard the important role of the interlinking of local solutions supporting local practices.

Consider infrastructures such as the electricity networks, or the Internet. Looking at them as purely technical infrastructures, which have to be managed according to pre-specified plans, would miss their second nature as heterogeneous collections of technical components, humans, and institutions. These include the purely technical system, its designers and their supporting organization, and regulating bodies. Such systems are both socially constructed and society shaping. They are dynamic actor networks.

As an illustration, consider how the concepts introduced thus far are relevant in interpreting some of the key features of the Internet. The development of the Internet is a story of painstaking alignment involving at different times: software companies; military agencies; research laboratories; competing technical solutions; and so on. Inventors, engineers, scientists, managers, and subsequently politicians and businessmen have shown interest in the growth and durability of the network. During its early development as ARPANET, both military goals and the requirements and values of the academic community (such as collegiality, decentralization, and open exchange) migrated into some of the key technical specifications of the network: packet switching and the TCP/IP protocols. These technical choices were to support the idea of a resilient, decentralized network that was appealing, though for different reasons, to the military sponsors and the academic and industrial designers. Once values are successfully inscribed, large technical systems, as a result of alignment, tend to acquire style and momentum as they mature. The Internet, once key technical solutions were implemented, acquired direction and displayed an impressive rate of growth. And as it grows it becomes even more attractive for new users to adopt it. The concept of momentum is closely related to the self-reinforcing processes at the core of the economics of standards. Reverse salients can play an important role in the next stages of the development of infrastructures. Reverse salients are those elements that are lagging behind and impeding the further development of the whole system. Dealing with the reverse salient brings major jumps, and sometimes radical shifts, in the direction and evolution of the infrastructure. Thus, for example, TCP/IP addressed brilliantly the reverse salient of letting different networks link with each other, and brought the explosive growth of Internet usage.

Exploiting existing installed bases as underlying infrastructures, translating them into allies, will always be important when establishing new infrastructures. To make an infrastructure grow, it needs to be planted in fertile soil. The potential success of this strategy is illustrated by the way the World Wide Web has been designed to build on the existing Internet.

Adaptation is a response to different environments and adaptation to environments culminates in a unique *style*. Style is determined not only by technology, but also by culture, bodies of regulation, habits, and mindsets.

Finally, infrastructures embody a representation of the functioning of the organizations they support, especially when they are deployed jointly with BPR. In other words, infrastructures are not just made of networks, data flows, and work procedures, but also are embodiments, or vehicles, of emerging modes of work organization, of new cognitive imageries and institutional arrangements (recall the notion of inscription). More specifically, they interact with both the structural and institutional arrangements associated with a given division of labour, and the assumptions, frames, and mental images people hold while routinely enacting and practising that specific division of labour: infrastructures are immersed in and nurture cognitive, organizational, and institutional ecologies.

Consequently, infrastructures can be regarded as formative contexts, that is, not just as sets of hardware and software but as sets of the pre-existing institutional arrangements, cognitive frames, and imageries that actors bring to, and routinely enact in, a situation of action. As such, they also constitute the background condition for action, enforcing constraints, giving direction and meaning, and setting the range of opportunities for undertaking new actions. An infrastructure as a formative context will then be able to shape both the organization of work and the set of social scripts which govern the invention of alternative forms of work, the future ways of problem solving and conflict resolution, the revision of the existing institutional arrangements, and the plans for their further transformation. For example, ARPANET in its early days changed the way computer scientists who were using it worked and collaborated. The development of new languages like Common LISP was made possible by the new means of communication, file exchange, etc. The infrastructure triggers reflexivity, thus new projects and developments have been made possible in the very field of networking and computing as a direct result. The development of the operating system Linux and the growth of the open source movement are other outcomes of such reflexivity. Thus, far from being a purely technical device, the infrastructure becomes the new formative context that moulds and constrains new and old cognitive processes and practices.

Infrastructure as *Gestell*

We now want to come full circle around the central notion of information infrastructure and its relevant agendas. Surprisingly, our initial case, CRM, has its roots in writings and theories that go beyond economics and the social sciences right into philosophy: namely, the work of Winograd and Flores (1987), who were among the first to look at computers and networks as tools to support action during breakdowns. Within the CRM concept one can identify those activities that are required to complete a transaction by overcoming various forms of breakdown. Winograd and Flores pick many of their ideas, such as dealing with breakdowns, technology as a tool, and engagement in a transaction, from an original reading of Heidegger's phenomenological enquiry. In what follows, we harness Heidegger's ideas on technology, not really utilized by the two authors, to throw a new light on the essence of infrastructure and propose alternative ways to dwell next to it. Another industrial example, very different from CRM, will be presented to show such alternative ideas at work.

To begin with, for Heidegger the essence of modern technology is denoted by the German word *Gestell*. *Gestell* means skeleton, frame, or shelf and the term *Untergestell* means chassis and infrastructure (a light physical support).

But the German philosopher uses the term in a new sense. *Gestell* is composed of a prefix *Ge* and the word *Stelle* derived from the verb *stellen*. *Ge*, in German, is the prefix that denotes reunion, gathering, or collecting and reassembling (think of *Ge-sellschaft* for society; or *Ge-meinschaft* for community; or *Ge-birge* for mountain (*Bergen*) chain). *Stelle* and *stellen* have a variety of meanings: the noun means place, spot, location; the verb means generically put, place, stand, set, arrange, regulate, provide, order, etc.

Thus, *Gestell* means literally the reunion of the placing, arranging, regulating, ordering—but of what, and how? And what has such a reunion to do with technology? First, Heidegger puts forward the idea that the essence of technology is not something technical, something linked to the more or less fascinating technical aspects of highly sophisticated tools for production, transport, communication, or power generation. The essence of technology as a phenomenon lies beyond such appearances. A phenomenon is what shows in itself beyond first appearance (see Methodological Appendix). Heidegger approaches the phenomenon of modern technology by unveiling and letting be seen what may lie behind the fabulous appearances of modern technology. He does it from two slightly different angles around the crucial definition of *Gestell*.

Think for a moment: despite the power of modern technology to shorten distances, things still remain far for us. 'All the mastering of farness does not deliver any proximity, rather we experience the world as an undifferentiated without-distance' (Heidegger 1994). Such a without-distance has definitely a place: it constitutes the stock (*Bestand*) of all that is existing (is present). What supplies this stock of undifferentiated resources that represent the world as experienced by the modern human being? It is the supplying itself, *bestellen*, that is the infinite chain of actions of ordering, requiring, demand, and supply.

'The forester who measures the felled timber in the woods . . . is today ordered by the industry that produces commercial woods, whether he knows it or not. He is made subordinate to the orderability of cellulose, which for its part is challenged forth by the need for paper, which is then delivered to newspapers and illus-trated magazines. The latter, in their turn, set public opinion to swallowing what is printed, so that a set configuration of opin-ion becomes available on demand' (Heidegger 1978).

People, far from being the masters of this enchaining process, are—under various forms as workers, managers, or citizens who read the newspapers—employed (ordered and organized) by this process, thus becoming themselves parts of that stock or standing reserve. This circulation process is self-feeding and leads to nothing else than its perpetuation. It becomes so universal as to embrace the world, nature, history, and the destiny of mankind.

The gathering of the multiple actions of ordering and their enchainment is called *Gestell*.[1] *Gestell* captures all that is extant and makes it available through a stock to be put in circulation. Machines are built and applied, science generates new solutions that get converted into new systems and applications because of the *Gestell*, not the other way around. Nature itself loses the property of being an object (*Gegen-stand*) and becomes *Be-stand*, stock available to be exploited in this process of circulation.

It is because of this distortion in what we encounter as real (things, people, the world) that 'machines created by the tech-nology can only shorten distances, but at the same time do not bring about any proximity, precisely because the essence of the technology does not give access to proximity and farness', but just undifferentiated, average availability (Heidegger 1994).

Second, the essence of technology is to be an end: it is causal-ity. Causality should be understood in a broader sense, as a way

[1] The most frequent English translation of *Gestell* is 'the enframing'. Alternative translations are 'the com-positing' or simply 'com-posite': both suggestions aim at retaining the original meaning of *stellen* in English, though they seem (alas!) to lack the enframing effect.

of bringing forth, presenting. Hence, the essence of technology is its capacity to bring forth, to reveal.

The revealing that rules in modern technology is a challenging, setting upon resources, putting nature and man to demand to yield. It is a way of expediting, of driving on to the maximum yield. Such challenging happens in that the energy concealed in nature is unlocked, what is unlocked is transformed, what is transformed is stored up, what is stored up is in turn distributed, and what is distributed is switched about ever anew. Unlocking, transforming, storing, distributing, and switching about are ways of revealing. (Heidegger 1978)

We now turn to the contents of a possible Heideggerian agenda on infrastructure seen as *Gestell*, first appreciating how his perspective is very relevant for today's ICT infrastructures, though it was formulated more than half a century ago. The definition of *Gestell* as a reunion of the ordering process, or even literally as 'a frame that sets up', overcomes in a felicitous way the dichotomy between the structural, static, aspects of infrastructure and their dynamics. In *Gestell* both dimensions are hosted, while the term infrastructure seems to privilege the structural aspects only.

Secondly, the emphasis on the enchained processes of ordering highlights a paramount aspect of how infrastructure is conceived today in business. Networks are not only there to facilitate communication, but to reduce costs of transacting by supporting the alignment and interlocking of business processes within and between organizations. This is precisely the phenomenon of the intertwining of networks and computers as a layer on which enterprise packages (like ERP) can run to implement the linking of business processes and the management of workflows.

Thirdly, the self-feeding nature of such a process, and its reliance on planning and standards, are also included in the

Gestell. Standards, network externalities, imitation are all factors that contribute to the momentum of the self-feeding process of infrastructure development and diffusion.

More uncertain remains the role of characteristics such as installed base and irreversibility. They could be linked to the notion of *Bestand*, as standing reserve or stock, but in our modern vision of infrastructure it is the inertia of the successive accumulation of systems and applications that forms the outstanding feature of such a reserve. Heidegger, instead, seems to pinpoint the process of accumulation of resources made available as future input to the relentless ordering process. Of all the dynamics aspects of the technology, *Gestell* seems to give a priority to its accelerating, self-feeding aspects, while the study of infrastructures puts at least an equal emphasis on the inertial effects, seeing these as, in the end, the key determining factor of the quasi-autonomous nature of sophisticated system technologies in modern organizations.

Heidegger's ideas about what-to-do are developed in a further step of his enquiry into the essence of technology, namely around the notion of *Gefahr* (danger).

Gestell does not deliver the nearness to things. It does not deliver *the world* (that is, the 'there' where man's existence unfolds authentically). Instead, everything is just an undifferentiated standing reserve of resources ready to be deployed. *Gestell* becomes the world, but a world of a special kind, which can subsist only thanks to the oblivion of the authentic one. Through oblivion *Gestell* chases away the world. This chasing represents the essence of the *Gestell*'s danger. With a play of words, the danger is the essence of the essence of technology. However, there is no use in assuming a favourable or negative stance towards technology. Such stances would belong to the technical discourse on technology and do not deal with its essence. They always implicitly assume technology as a set of tools that can be good or bad, to be deployed in a positive or negative way. They address only the instrumental dimension of technology, that is, they adhere to the technical discourse on technology, missing that which is non-technical (non-instrumental) in the essence of technology.

What is the essence of the danger, then? It is *being* itself, the fact that *Gestell* comes to *represent* what 'is' and what 'is not'. The danger lies in the fact that *Gestell* delivers representations of all that subsists, and these become the real world. If one can talk about the domination of technology, one should speak of 'the domination of the essence of the technology that orders in its appropriating even and precisely the representations man makes about it . . . The essence of technology, the *Gestell*, carries out its own simulation' (Heidegger 1978, 1994). The outcome of such representing and simulating is the essence of the danger, able to encompass any discourse pro or con the technology and its effects. More radically, technology works outside the sphere of means and ends. It is not an object, or a tool among many. Rather, it becomes the hidden trait of all that today is taken as real. The danger, then, is not the destruction of nature or culture but certain totalizing kinds of practices—a levelling of our understanding of being.

Recall what we discussed in relation to the social studies of technology: the contextual and, at the same time, cognitive and institutional role of infrastructure. We can, then, appreciate the relevance of Heidegger's thought. Information infrastructures can, as formative contexts, shape not only the work routines, but also the ways people look at practices, consider them as being natural, and give them their overarching character of false necessity. Infrastructure becomes an essential factor shaping daily the taken-for-grantedness of organizational practices. Imaginings, world views, and reform initiatives, or new designs, are moulded by the subtle and hidden influence of infrastructures of formative contexts.

How to deal with the danger? Again, one should avoid falling into the seemingly easy role of being a romantic and reactionary critic of technology.

Gestell, having the power to enact a reality in which everything is a resource available to yield, would seem to leave little hope for any change, since any transformation or even debate about it would be somehow supervised and governed by the *Gestell* itself (again as a formative context). Heidegger does not agree with this conclusion, and submits, rather, that, where the greatest danger lies, also lies the closest opportunity for rescue. In a sudden, unpredictable moment, the moment of vision (see Chapter 8), the destiny of being can lead itself on other unexpected, and different, directions. These other directions will not put aside the technology, the essence of which still delivers reality through the *Gestell*, but such an essence might be able 'to heal itself, by finding its hidden truth' (Heidegger 1992). This shift of gears cannot have anything to do with a destiny that can be 'planned in a logical and historical way', nor as 'the outcome of a process of history that can be constructed or managed'. We have to learn a new style of thinking, a new disposition, commensurate with the healing of the destiny of being, the 'healing of the *Gestell*'; the new disposition will consist of human engagements, such as:

- *The ability to jump, or switch Gestalt.* The jump is needed to get out of calculative and instrumental thought, and approach domains where man can 'start asking the question of being anew'.
- *The importance of the moment of vision*, of that lightening that allows the insight in what it is, beyond the pervasive influence of the *Gestell*.

- *Releasement*, that is, a comportment toward technology which expresses a 'yes' and a 'no' simultaneously. We let technical devices enter our daily life, and at the same time leave them outside.
- *A new sense of responsibility*; the traditional notion of responsibility means to be in control of what comes from us. Releasement, instead, implies responsibility in accepting what is largely beyond our control, the unforeseen.
- *Openness to the mystery*, in order to remain open to the meaning hidden in technology, and the rehabilitation of astonishment at that which 'is'.
- *Valuing marginal practices*, the saving power of insignificant things, since they resist the drive for yield and efficiency (the domain of the *Gestell*).
- *Shifting fluctuations to centre stage*; taking up practices that are now at the margins of our culture and making them central, while de-emphasizing practices now central to our cultural self-understanding.

Coming full circle to the phenomenological underpinnings of a specific BPR programme, CRM, we have turned the initial management agenda, based on notions such as strategic intent, planning, alignment, and control, into a quite different one that highlights releasement, valuing fluctuations, openness to mystery, and sudden moments of vision.

A final case study

Our enquiry shows that Heidegger's questioning about the essence of modern technology is anything but outdated or irrelevant, despite the dramatic evolution of technology in the last half-century. The dynamic and static aspects of infrastructure in the economy and business organizations, and the far-reaching power of representation of any organizational activity through infrastructure, can benefit from a deeper understanding of many of the concepts put forward by phenomenology.

But one may wonder whether the questioning approach and its prescriptions just mentioned have any relevance in the world of business. We submit that agendas of this type are implemented more frequently than is usually suggested, and more so in knowledge-intensive organizations. We can look, for example, at how a corporate network infrastructure was developed and changed in a major pharmaceutical company, Hoffmann-La Roche, over a period of more than ten years. At the end of the 1980s the newly created Strategic Marketing function decided to implement the first company-wide network that would serve its own purposes. Strategic Marketing was created to streamline and centralize the marketing activities worldwide, in a corporate context where national affiliates retained strong autonomy: adaptation to local markets, and especially national regulations in healthcare, impeded the enactment of fully globalized processes.

Marketing a drug is knowledge intensive, as are most other activities in a pharmaceutical company. Knowledge is created in the course of developing a new product; knowledge emerges from the clinical trials and is consolidated in the New Drug Application; new knowledge is acquired and processed once the product is in use. Knowledge comes from various sources, inside and outside the company, and is continually gathered, processed, and communicated throughout the product life cycle. Strategic Marketing sifts, filters, accumulates, and distributes the knowledge that is necessary to market a global product. Strategic Marketing can intervene in and influence the local marketing activities only indirectly—namely, by providing the background knowledge that is essential to carry out effective marketing in each country. Such knowledge has many forms and supporting structures: training on the product features; information from clinical tests, both before the launch of the product and after; prescription strategies, and so on. Most of the knowledge consists of templates that have to be adapted, enriched, and modified locally.

In the second half of the 1980s Strategic Marketing oversaw the establishment of the first corporate network, which went under the name of MedNet, to support the new, centralized function of marketing, aimed at unifying the various national Roche affiliates. MedNet was established to increase the levels of global integration through standardization.

But after eight years, MedNet was discontinued. Its negative outcomes, especially the costs compared to its low level of use, dictated its end. The corporate network remained as a purely technical infrastructure, so the large investments were not completely lost. What was phased out, or better superseded, was the application portfolio. Brand new Internet and intranet applications took the place of MedNet.

The use of the Internet and intranets has not only brought about a different infrastructure layer; it has also introduced a newer style of networking and ICT use. Some of these modern features are rooted in MedNet; some have been brought in by the possibilities offered by the Internet. Perhaps most importantly, the later infrastructure is the carrier of a new vision of how to look at the business, at technology, and, more generally, at the customers and the outside environment.

Paradoxically, in this highly uncertain situation, the most favourable approach seems to be no plan/no strategy—just let web development and use unfold. The process is not mature enough to be managed; it is still in a discovery stage, and as such is nurtured and cultivated by the senior management of the marketing division. That the Internet and intranets are relatively cheap, or at least much less costly than MedNet, favours the hands-off, releasing attitude of top management. In the new practice, while a new context for doing business is possibly emerging, terms such as alignment or BPR simply have no meaning: they lack a relevant management context. Words such as drifting, *bricolage*, hospitality, and cultivation (see the next two chapters) seem to capture what is going on better, not only in the affiliates, but also in the headquarters.

The Roche case also exemplifies an alternative model of infrastructure development and diffusion from the one of top-down, strategic alignment (see Chapter 2). With this new approach there is no strong top-down direction, but rather releasement; no alignment by *fiat*, but rather a loose coupling between local context and technology initiatives. Thus, the infrastructure expands by the decentralized linking of local initiatives that are born as spin-offs of headquarters' initiatives. The latter constitute a reference model for imitation, and provide the content, so that local websites can be built, initially with minimal (but critical mass) content. The grass-roots initiatives enjoy two key features: they are local (and sometimes expressed in local language—while MedNet was always at fault in this respect), and they retain a link with the headquarters' content. Navigation allows the user to cross local/global boundaries seamlessly, though in practice this is not done as frequently as might be expected.

The power of the periphery, the affiliates, is harnessed to support the diffusion of the infrastructure, not as a source of resistance. The process of infrastructure building becomes self-reinforcing, albeit to some extent centrifugal. All this seems to fit neatly with the way knowledge is managed in marketing activities: key knowledge is created centrally around the development of the product, but much complementary knowledge is generated and resides close to local markets. The use of the Internet and the intranet as a technical infrastructure, and the new management approach—a mixture of releasement and cultivating strategies—seem to fit the loosely coupled nature of the distribution of knowledge within and across the business. It is a case of a surprising alignment and fit through the *decoupling* of tools, processes, and local and central practices, in the aftermath of the hard and costly lesson learned through MedNet: the impossibility of enforced, top-down alignment of the infrastructure.

5

Dérive

Hopefully the previous chapters have increased our appetite to explore the issue of the role of ICTs in modern organizations. We may put forward more specific questions, at this point, such as: are applications like groupware supporting teamwork successfully? Do these systems help to delayer managerial hierarchies? Do ERP systems streamline business processes? Do global infrastructures contribute to business efficiency and integration? Do these systems actually increase productivity and sharpen managerial control? Is it true that they lead to a decrease in transaction costs and the creation of new markets, as maintained both by theory and by the advocates of e-commerce?

To all these and similar questions one can give largely positive answers, and acquiesce in the belief that a few of the multiple,

The materials for this chapter come from three main sources: C. U. Ciborra (1996), 'What does groupware mean?', in C. U. Ciborra (ed.), *Groupware and Teamwork* (Chichester: John Wiley); C. U. Ciborra and O. Hanseth (2001), 'Introduction', in C. U. Ciborra *et al.*, *From Control to Drift* (Oxford: Oxford University Press): 1–11; C. U. Ciborra (2000), 'Drifting', in K. Braa, C. Sorensen, and B. Dahlbom (eds.), *Planet Internet* (Lund: Studentlitteratur): 185–96.

apparent facets of the new technology in use have been captured. At the limit, one could choose to measure quantitatively
all the impacts above, in order to perfect further our ability to
establish effective governance of modern technology.

At the same time, however, a closer look at what happens in
organizations reveals ubiquitous, puzzling processes of tinkering, hacking, and improvisation around the implementation and
use of new technology (see Chapter 3). Given the naturally
occurring or triggered learning processes that surround any
innovation, and the unavoidable breakdowns that punctuate the
trajectory of any complex system when deployed, one can char-
acterize the overall consequence of these practices and events
with the simple explanation that the technology does not seem
to work completely according to plan. This phenomenon is
becoming so noteworthy that new perspectives, like actor network theory (see Chapter 4), are being introduced in the IS field
to capture better the recalcitrance, or even the full agency—and
in any case the lack of docility—of ICTs. In the present chapter
we will not pursue further the radical view of technology as
being endowed with independent action, or even intentions.
More modestly, we want to allow ourselves a middle ground,
and dwell on all the emerging symptoms just mentioned, reflecting on the idea that one of the main characteristics of ICT as a
modern phenomenon in organizations and society is that it is
á la dérive: the information infrastructure might have enhancing
effects but it also drifts.

Through such reflection we encounter the phenomenological
middle ground where intentions of humans and non-humans
mingle and blur; where learning and recalcitrance, hacking and
inertia show up simultaneously. This is the station to pause and
weigh the far-reaching and unpredictable trajectories of modern
technology in organizations. A middle ground where we can

whisper firmly and crisply what we have never been able to confess, but we very rapidly concluded: that we can only fully figure out the meaning of new technology in businesses and institutions after the fact; and that we plainly have to live with such impossibility and such a state of ignorance. All this offers a tremendous opportunity to finally rid ourselves of naïve models and frameworks, and explore anew the still uncharted grounds of our relationship with technology.

True stories, again

At the end of a qualitative empirical study of groupware applications in a few large multinationals, the researchers found that the development and use of groupware in large, complex organizations is variable and context specific (Ciborra 1996). In particular, in almost all the cases considered, groupware presented itself as a technology that tended to drift when put to use. Drifting describes a slight, or sometimes significant, shift of the role and function in concrete situations of usage, compared to the planned, pre-defined, and assigned objectives and requirements that the technology is called upon to perform (irrespective of who plans or defines them, whether they are users, sponsors, specialists, vendors, or consultants). Table 5.1 lists the main instances of drifting unveiled in the companies studied, for each application. Drifting should not be considered as a negative phenomenon *per se*: it can occur for both applications that are seen as successes and those that are not. For example, a large GDSS system within the World Bank led to a surprising result in use. The initial goal of the application was to improve the collective decision making during important policy meetings within the complex environment of the Bank, where different cultures and

Table 5.1 *Drifting effects*

Company	Application/ system	Drifting effects
Zeta	Lotus Notes	• new ways of knowledge sharing • emergence of new intermediary roles • new norms of reciprocal help over the network
Roche	Dedicated corporate network Videoconferencing Lotus Notes	• media substitution • high centralization
Unilever	Lotus Notes applications	• bypassing existing routines • too much formalization • opportunistic games • media substitution
Telecom	Lotus Notes	• lack of knowledge sharing • inter-functional rivalry
EDF	Lotus Notes	• under-utilization of the system due to substitute media • inter-functional rivalry
World Bank	GDSS	• lack of use for collective decision making • use as a group focusing support
Insurance	Lotus Notes	• serendipitous development

Source: Adapted from Ciborra (1996).

political interests have to converge on highly sensitive investment decisions. The GDSS systems offered a range of possible
uses, besides the voting functionality. Such variety fitted well
with the daily dynamics at the Bank, highly sensitive decision
making usually being prepared outside the meetings where the
decision had to be formally deliberated. Users of the GDSS
tacitly agreed to keep the present practice, while using the facility only to brainstorm and focus on issues. So, the system was
successful in being heavily used, but *not* as a decision support
system.

In other cases, like EDF and Unilever, the researchers
observed that key features and functionalities of the groupware
application were being bypassed by the intended users. The drifting phenomenon also captures the sequence of ad-hoc adjustments that punctuate the evolution of the customer support at
Zeta or the *bricolage* in the development of the Lotus Notes
application at Insurance.

Drifting can be looked at as the outcome of two intertwined
processes. One is given by the openness of the technology, its
plasticity in response to the re-inventions carried out by users
and specialists, who gradually learn to discover and exploit features, affordances, and potentialities of systems. On the other
hand, there is the sheer unfolding of the actors' being-in-the-
workflow and the continuous stream of interventions, tinkering,
and improvisations that colour perceptions of the entire system
life cycle (see Chapter 3).

The outcome of these two processes led the researchers to the
surprising conclusion that 'what groupware is' can only be
ascertained *in situ*, when the matching between plasticity of the
artefact and the multiform practices of the actors involved takes
place. Such a matching is open, situated, and continuously
unfolding.

The researchers conclude further that technology drifting seems to be a widespread process. The various instances of drifting unveil a variety of learning processes taking place around the innovation and punctuating its internalization into the organization. Such processes may range from improvisation to radical reform; additionally, they tend to occur in a fragmented, loose manner. Hence, drifting better captures the essence of groupware implementation than does evolution. Drifting seems to lie outside the scope of control of the various actors; it consists of small and big surprises, discoveries and blockages, opportunistic turns and vicious circles. As a consequence many groupware applications are not implemented at a speed consistent with the pace of business transformation (for example, Roche); others make big jumps, but in unexpected directions (for example, the World Bank); still others zigzag.

Drifting and systems development

The reader should be able to guess at this point that the present chapter is also about the way the obvious becomes hidden during the implementation and use of new technologies: in other words technology very often seems to shift away, to a greater or lesser extent, from the designed tracks and pre-defined goals. This is very common, but also frequently forgotten or avoided: it is the unthinkable that is never mentioned, not even during those would-be creative management training sessions dedicated to 'thinking the unthinkable'. It so frequently and fastidiously invades the everyday world of a project that it represents the last thing one wants to talk about, let alone reflect upon, especially when trying out ways of improving the development and use of systems. The more that systems and applications are distributed, multifaceted, and a-centred (as in the case of the Internet), the more this phenomenon will be ubiquitous and momentous.

Systems development methodologies maintain that applications should be aligned with their initial specifications. They are horrified by fluctuations and deviations; therefore, they strive to keep them in check through systematic monitoring, feedback, and learning. Somehow, though, shift and drift in systems development and use always succeed in creeping in, and subtract value from the methodologies, contributing to the frustration and scepticism amongst conscientious practitioners. We choose, instead, to be funky once again and celebrate deviations and mismatches: looking at them positively as a source of innovation, or simply as that existential dirt which is destined to corrupt the neat but idealized picture of any systems development project. Chapter 3 showed that the use of applications is always shaped by hacks, short cuts, and twists, or punctuated through unpredictable processes of re-invention. Drifting is the result of these processes—ranging from sabotage, to passive resistance, to learning-by-doing, to astonishing micro discoveries and radical shifts—or of plain serendipity. In these processes, usage, maintenance and redevelopment, and continuous, or sometimes fortuitous, improvements take place simultaneously. In a corporate world without drifting, service technicians would have no war stories to swap, coffee machine chats would only deal with football, cars, and dirty jokes, and office automation ethnographers would be out of work.

More generally, an insight into the drifting of technology needs to recombine, on a different basis, the theory and practice of systems development and use. Schön (1983) suggests that those who promote or adhere to methodologies have a view from the high ground, and tend to ignore what goes on in the (daily) swamp of actual projects. Drifting characterizes life in the swamp. We want to put forward a few systematic considerations on the swamp of development and use: a first attempt towards a swampy theory of information systems implementation.

A general model

As mentioned above, drifting is about situated technology, to use a perspective with a feminist slant. It is about technology in use, as experienced and seen from the swamp of contingent situations and practices, and not from the crisp, crystal-clear high ground of method. A model of drifting must be based on those modes of operation that make up the fabric of the world of practice. Drifting denotes the dynamics of an encounter, of pasting up a hybrid composed of technology, organizations, people, and artefacts. Drifting is a way to capture the unfolding of the intrinsic openness of such an encounter. The fluid territory on which such an unfolding takes place is the swamp of everyday life in organizations.

To begin our venture into the swamp, drifting reveals that technology and artefacts possess affordances. Norman (1988) defines affordance in terms of the 'psychology of everyday things': what people perceive artefacts can do. Affordance captures those fundamental properties that seem to tell us what the things can do for us. Actually, Heidegger (1962) suggested earlier that our knowledge and basic way of encountering the world are obtained through the use of, and not the scientific description of, objects. The world is a never-ending assemblage of affordances, rather than things or decontextualized objects: it is the realm of the how-to.

In such a world of everyday life, people move around like insects, relying on an infinite variety of coping and care tactics.

These are micro-interventions consisting of studied *bricolage* or rapid improvisations, dictated more by impromptu, local existential projections and designs than by any long-range strategy (see Chapter 8).

Tactics stay glued to things and situations: they allow for a detailed reading of affordances and the discovery of new ones. Tactics stick to the terrain: they seldom raise their gaze out of the swamp. By staying in intimate contact with things and situations they discover the hidden dispositions of artefacts and organization structures (see Chapter 7), their intrinsic potential for action. Artefacts and people become the springboard for new actions, for further tactics: the reregistering of the world through the disclosure of the dispositions (hidden affordances) keeps the everyday world moving, and makes *bricolage* and improvisation into sources of innovation. Matching visible and invisible affordances with tactics leads to new uses: the re-invention of artefacts and technologies and their shifting away from the pre-assigned uses. The result is drifting. Drift is thus the outcome of the match between two agents: technology-possessing affordances; and humans in their various roles of sponsor, user, and designer.

The model outlined so far identifies drifting as the outcome of a matching between an open technology and situated humans' interventions of use. The danger of such a model is to replicate, though in a shifted manner, the sequence typical of planned implementation: goals are guided by activities, which lead to outcomes. In drifting, the difference would be that activities are distinct from those originally envisaged and driven by different goals. The reconstruction of drifting would, then, amount to the identification of the goals, actors, and their interventions, which may explain why a given system turned out to be used differently from the initial plans. Drifting would be regarded as the outcome of an alternative agenda (and an alternative power group) to the one dictated by explicit plans and methods. The task for the analyst or consultant would be to identify and harness the contents and dynamics of such an alternative agenda.

Thus we can see technologies drift because one set of goals/activities replaces another. We submit, however, that drifting is not just planning and acting according to different goals, or the unfolding of an alternative strategy. Drift can hardly be referred to as a plan, even an alternative one: drift chases the plan away while still being complementary to it.

This emphasizes that we are confronted with the methodological challenge of interpreting drifting in the terms of the swamp and not of the high ground. The human dimension of drifting belongs to the world of everyday practices: ubiquitous but anonymous; made of ruses and short cuts; improvised; marginal; relying on age-old, timeless skills. And as such it needs to be captured.

Swampy time and space

Plans and methods belong to the high ground dominated by the notion of space, where time is clock time (as the fourth dimension complementing the ones of three-dimensional physical space, see Chapter 8). It is in this space that the flow diagrams, and the activity and sequence maps, are currently expressed.

In contrast, drifting is made of *bricolage* and improvisation. The latter activities can hardly be hosted by (find a meaningful context in) the large, chilly spaces of the high ground. They are local, short, and sudden, and do not exist outside the specific situation where they appear. They belong to the opaque, shapeless (boxless) world of the swamp, where time is fluid or out of joint.

Procedures unfold according to clock time and their execution relies upon pre-packaged knowledge, lying in front of the actor as deadlines, goals, and planned actions.

On the other hand, Chapter 8 will show that improvisation occurs in the *Augenblick*, the moment of vision, and is an expression of deep-seated memory or experience of the actor. Procedures can be ordered, sequenced, and reproduced. Improvisations can only be recounted as stories which have principally an inspiring value, cannot be reproduced, and actually belong only to the recounting of the story itself: to its situated, performed narrative.

Let us consider in more detail the contrast between these two approaches. Models and methods belong to those strategies (of military, more than scientific, origin) that focus on the space dimension in multiple ways, since they want to pursue:

- *neatness*: by establishing proper space for activities to be performed in an orderly fashion;
- *structure*: by elaborating theoretical places (systems and totalizing discourses);
- *articulation*: by identifying appropriate physical spaces, from the overhead transparencies to the screens estate throughout the office buildings and laboratories.

In this way, 'they attempt to reduce temporal relations to spatial ones, through the analytical attribution of a proper place to each particular element and through the combinatory organization of the movements specific to units or groups of units' (De Certeau 1988).

On the other hand, tactics, ruses, improvisations, of which drifting is the product and outcome, are *contingent* procedures indexed by the here and now, and meaningless outside a specific time-tagged situation. Given a linear, pre-planned procedure made of a sequence of actions, tactics are precisely those scrambling interventions, multiple variations, those fleeting creative acts that transform the expected neutral situation into a situation perceived as favourable or pleasant.

Those plans and stable procedures that models and methods comprise want to defy time by their robustness and stability: they announce organizations as pyramids. Tactics, instead, are rapidly moving, their mobile interventions being dictated by and forcing the seizing of the moment. The former bet on space and order; the latter on the appropriate time and the contingent situation. The former adhere to a solid track. The latter are condemned to be ephemeral and transformative.

The practices found in drifting also tell us something about knowledge in organizations. Drifting stems from those mundane, invisible practices that, compared to the crisp world of procedure and method, in a way represent the dark, nocturnal side of organizational work. They are intelligent practices: the expression of a practical intelligence (Scribner 1984). Far from the by now conventional distinction between tacit and explicit knowledge, practical intelligence is the *metis* of the Greek—the intelligence of the octopus: flexible, polymorphic, ambiguous, oblique, twisted, circular. In one word; it is the opposite of the straight, direct, rigid, and univocal knowledge embedded in method. To orient oneself in the complex and changing world, when dealing with forces that are too strong to be fully controlled, one needs to leverage the situation at hand, by *détournement*, false moves, wavering behaviour, never facing such forces up front, but accomplishing with a sudden move (improvisation) the project at hand.

To be sure, these two modes of operating are clearly, and have been, coexisting and complementary, at the same time excluding each other (BPR wanting to eliminate improvisation . . .) and supporting each other (tactics grow like lichens over procedures and models when put in use). Large systems and models take off only if surrounded by a regimen of tactics that fills the gaps between the complex formalized procedures and the floating world of complex organizations and turbulent economies.

Global consequences

Drifting phenomena have been found also when studying the deployment and use of large information infrastructures in global companies (see Chapter 4). Despite attempts by multinational companies to adhere to the tenets of BPR and strategic alignment of ICT in their pursuit of globalization and centralization strategies, drifting abounds. For example, in an international product division of a large Norwegian company the implementation of a complex SAP application gradually unveiled the dynamic and uncontrollable role of the technology. Given the high degree of complexity of the new infrastructure, its diffusion across the different national affiliates can only take place through local adaptations and compromises. Eventually the sum of these adaptations carried out in pursuit of enacting a common standard leads to an opposite result: the local instantiations are so many that a common standard remains an elusive goal, while the penetration of the technology progressively ossifies the work procedures. As a result, local autonomies are after all preserved; the common standard remains a yet-to-be-achieved goal, with a technology imposing on the human agents its own constraints, all this outside any managerial or technical plan.

In the context of globalization, drifting acquires more general contours. The modes of operation and the tactics which make up the human side of drifting are engaged in creative uses of time (see above and Chapter 8), but they tend to remain spatially confined by the communities of practices (the team; the department; the affiliate). However, the extension of infrastructures and the spread of large applications and methodologies connect communities and cross boundaries to an extent never needed before. In this respect, De Certeau (1988) again remarks that, 'Tactics are more and more going off their tracks. Cut loose from their traditional communities that circumscribed their functioning, they have begun to wander everywhere . . . [hence] Consumers are transformed into immigrants . . . [and] there is no longer an elsewhere.' It is this phenomenon that made Giddens (1990) suggest, a few years later, that the side effects provoked by technology and organizations constitute the supreme factors that make the modern, global world go round.

The upshot is that in a context where drifting and side effects are both unavoidable and momentous, the complex process of wiring the corporation cannot be understood, let alone managed, by applying approaches that were effective for mechanical organizations, and assembly-line types of technologies and processes. Machine-like bureaucracies are highly decomposable along hierarchical lines. In contrast, information infrastructures are deployed within a web of externalities and interdependencies (see the ideas contained in the economic agenda reported in Chapter 4). It is too simplistic to cut through such interdependencies with the old, industrial-age models shaped by the principle of functional, hierarchical decomposition.

Globalization as enabled by technology is a kaleidoscopic process. Corporate information infrastructures are puzzles, or more aptly collages, and so are the design and implementation processes that lead to their construction and operation. In their turn, such puzzles and collages are embedded in larger, contextual puzzles and collages. Interdependence, intricacy, and interweaving of people, systems, and processes are the culture bed of the information infrastructure. Patching, alignment of heterogeneous actors, and *bricolage* are the most frequent approaches found in actual business practice, irrespective of whether management was planning or strategy oriented, or inclined to react to contingencies.

Here, our attention to the drifting phenomena makes us diverge again from the management literature. The latter easily acknowledges that the state of infrastructures in many companies resembles a somewhat messy collage, as a result of deals, improvisations, and layers of sedimentation. But this is seen as a state of affairs that should be abandoned in favour of a more integrated and controlled approach aimed at streamlining the infrastructure, fitting it into the corporate strategy, and extracting more value from it. In this view, the collage is there, but it is bad, dysfunctional, and ought to be avoided. The value added by the management models and methods would consist precisely in moving infrastructure from a thrown-together institutional backbone to a value-generating, integrated set of technologies, applications, and processes. Substantial gains in productivity are promised, together with the general shared and legitimate concern for achieving an increasing level of control on a resource that is complex, expensive, enduring, and critical for running a business in the information society.

Indeed control is an overarching issue for business organizations. Industrial technologies and organizational forms have had as their main objective the creation of more advanced governance instruments that enable us to enhance and extend our mastery over processes in society and nature. Correspondingly, most of the management literature continues to provide models and tools to enhance and support control over business processes—production, distribution, marketing, sales, and so on.

But effective control is difficult to achieve. Nature, society, and the economy have always been unpredictable and uncontrollable. Although technology allows us to sharpen our control capabilities, we seem to end up deploying technology to create a world more difficult to master (see the dynamics of *Gestell*, in Chapter 4). This is also what globalization is all about: not just more extensive transactions or higher cross-border investments. We experience control in the age of globalization as more limited than ever. We are creating new global phenomena (global warming and greenhouse effects, nuclear threats, global production processes, and so on) that we are able to master only in part. Although information infrastructures appear to be important instruments for governing global phenomena, they possess ambiguities which make their eventual outcome difficult to determine. Consequently, they may serve to curb our control capabilities just as much as they enhance them.

The map contained in Fig. 5.1 offers a crude description of the vicious circles that businesses follow from the tight, top-down control of the ICT infrastructure to the actual drift of the infrastructure itself. To be sure, the formative context within which this circle subsists is centred on the credo of 'management is control'. Implementation tactics, the power of the installed base, and the sheer complexity of the new infrastructure are all factors that make for a different outcome: drift.

Individual and organizational limits to learning and the power of the pre-existing formative context make it very difficult for businesses to escape from the vicious circles. On the contrary, they reinforce the perceived need for even more control: this never-ending need and its consequences seem to be the hidden engine of our modern world of business and technology: a runaway world (Giddens 1990).

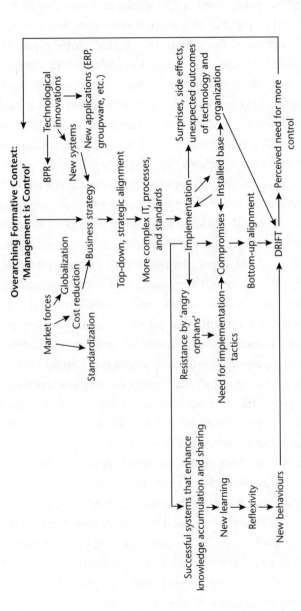

Figure 5.1 Mapping the dynamics of an ICT infrastructure.

Adapted from Ciborra *et al.* (2001).

Our storyline, then, unfolds differently, in a way that is perhaps more perplexing, but also more open-ended. Since we are successful in operating through more complex, global organizations and are able to learn new things by tapping wider amounts of information, the number of new opportunities emerging is growing larger and larger, and all our previous belief in planning and control processes and systems is becoming outdated at an increasing speed. Drifting is a side effect of our control actions and learning processes (reflexivity). The information infrastructure, being one of the backbones of such processes, is a true citizen of the runaway world. Hence, it shares its main surprising aspects: it is open-ended and in part out of control. The management literature privileges the ideal image of organizations as pyramids; the orderly, top-down process of strategic planning; the prescriptions on how to measure and control resources. Thus, it reproduces within organizations the fundamental principles of positivistic thinking that powered the industrial world for more than a century: the centrality of measure and control; technology as a powerful set of tools augmenting human action and thinking; the need to pull the messy everyday world towards an almost geometrical or mechanical view of the business organization, characterized by measurable and representable forces, linkages, and dynamics. The empirical studies referred to so far suggest that those principles which governed the emergence of the industrial society cannot be applied to the information society, without significantly changing those principles. The terms may be the same, because one society gave birth to the other, one economy still feeds upon and is fed by the others. However, their deep meaning can diverge radically.

Drifting makes us appreciate that globalization is not only about the architecture of transactions and the standardization of interfaces; it is a runaway process. Correspondingly, the corporate context should be looked at as a runaway learning organization: dynamic and unpredictable. This leads to a paradoxical implication: the main side effects of globalization will be higher risk and less control. Beck's (1992) notion of risk society is important in this respect. The ubiquitous integration at the core of the ongoing modernization and globalization processes leads to an increasing importance of unintended side effects. All actions imply side effects, and greater integration implies that side effects travel faster and longer: their role widens. More than anything globalization should be regarded as the globalization of unintended and unpredictable side effects. This leads further to higher levels of unpredictability and risk: more generally, to a risk society.

Finally, we can note how the study of drifting, together with the exploration of the concept of *Gestell*, points to an emerging definition of technology. ICT as an encompassing infrastructure can now be looked at as the unfolding process of connecting and scripting (enframing), and a receptacle of moves (invention, design, cultivation, modes of use) and constraints, enacted by humans and non-humans, among whom the accumulated state of the previous process stages, i.e. the installed base, is a powerful one.

The question now is: how should we relate to such complex and dynamic infrastructures? Obviously, and once again, the old methods do not apply.

6

Xenia

Since ancient times, hospitality has been an important (even sacred) institution able to establish a much needed bridge between the nomads, the pilgrims, the strangers, and the settlers of the cities; more generally, between the inside and the outside of a settlement, a house, or a persona. Hospitality has worked over the centuries as a time-economizing institution: it is an institutional device to cut down the time needed to merge cultures, and to integrate alien mindsets and costumes. Hospitality can precipitate the turning of an ephemeral contact into a relationship that has the look (and the feel) of long acquaintance.

If we draw the full consequences of imagining an economy filled by ephemeral, knowledge-based organizations, able to move, disassemble, and reconfigure themselves to meet customer demands and technological innovations (see Chapter 7) we need to shift gears, and drop the language of planning, controlling,

The chapter was originally published as C. U. Ciborra (1999), 'Hospitality and IT', in F. Ljunberg (ed.), *Informatics in the Next Millennium* (Lund: Studentlitteratur): 161–76.

and measuring through which organizations, teams, and projects have been managed so far. That language stems from heavy and slow-changing industries and infrastructures, driven by concerns for static economies of scale. A new language for the age of dynamic efficiency is needed urgently. Further, an enquiry into the phenomenon of hospitality can introduce a genre of discourse closer to the life world with which to frame the relationship between technology, organizations, and people.

In Chapter 2, I illustrated how the way in which such a relationship is usually managed, for example by applying various structured methodologies, may create severe obstacles to facing the challenges of building and living in nomadic organizations with ever changing routines and structures. Here we will point out how, by skipping over issues like hospitality and adopting the scientific mode of discourse, systems methodologies turn themselves away from everyday human dealings with technology, and find a (shaky) refuge in general and abstract dispositions and norms. They dislodge the problem of human existence out of the development and use of systems, and attempt to fill this ontological gap with the appearances of logic, objects, standards, and measurements, to, as concerned practitioners all over the world can testify, little avail.

As already mentioned, the abstract and sanitized models and methods which represent today's prevailing forms of dogmatism need to be abandoned in favour of a new constellation of issues, words, and understanding, referring in particular to existential dimensions, such as life world, identity, and commitment.

The notion of hospitality offers an opportunity to explore anew the complexities of designing, developing, and implementing systems in organizations. A fresh agenda emerges which appears more consistent with recent findings from the social studies of technology; specifically the symmetry between humans and non-humans proposed by the social studies of technology mentioned in Chapter 4. Last but not least, we should be able to contrast the idea of hospitality with the ones commonly presumed to prevail in the organizational landscape of the future, such as economic exchanges taking place through markets.

A methodological wasteland

Bracket what you think you know about systems development and implementation processes *before* jumping in to find better ways of improving, streamlining, and re-engineering them. It is a first step to grasping systems development (and more generally our relationship to technology and design) from a phenomenological perspective. Bracketing what we tend to take for granted allows us to dispose of those self-evident appearances which often serve to obscure our understanding of the phenomenon under investigation and discourage any alternative approaches (see Methodological Appendix). Appearances, such as goals, plans, control procedures, measurement techniques, and the vaguely pervasive and seductive notion of technology as a familiar, domesticated tool, are what the phenomenon under consideration is not.

Instead, take time to reflect upon the puzzling evidence provided by the continuous apparitions which punctuate any systems development effort and system in use: unexpected consequences; drifting of the technology; frequent tinkering and improvisations coupled with partial acceptance of methodologies, including implicit resistance to continuous improvement methodologies, if not open critique of their scientific foundations put forward even by specialists and practitioners. Such apparitions are symptoms of a *malaise* in the current ways of

understanding and approaching systems development and use.
Here is a working list of some related pathologies.

- *Excessive idealism*: the gap between daily tinkering and
  bricolage on the one hand, and the unfulfilled ambitions
  of abstract methodologies on the other, creates disillusion
  and frustration, if not cynicism, among practitioners.

- *Speed and oblivion*: in many organizations the relentless
  sequence of projects and development initiatives seems
  to go nowhere. New master plans, accompanied by new
  methods, follow each other at an increasing pace. The new
  supplant the old, even though their implementation is still
  incomplete. The impacts and *raison d'être* of the latter get
  quickly forgotten. Learning is scant and time becomes yet
  another severe constraint that hinders fatally the orderly
  application of any method.

- *Carbon copy projects*: new projects and methods are forced
  from the outside and are followed disgruntledly as yet
  another bureaucratic procedure: instead of action, one finds
  perfunctory compliance.

- *Narcissism*: in order to overcome passivity, loss of meaning,
  and drifting, strong actors, champions, or leaders become
  the main driving force to keep the methodologies alive. The
  approaches, as neutral and scientific, can be operationalized
  only through a quasi-charismatic leadership style, which lies
  at the far end of the spectrum of the scientific methodological paradigm. Hence, a double bind paralyses the practitioner: is it systematic rigour or forceful leadership?

- *Technical bias*: projects get encapsulated into a maze of grids,
  charts, measures, and spreadsheets. Any creativity and
  personal touch are evicted: the concern for the careful management of the means takes over any consideration for
  the—uncertain, complex, and risky—ends.

- *Totalitarian bias*: the projects drastically simplify reality, eliminating complexity and risk, for example by using apparently neutral measures extracted from questionnaires. This creates a gap between the life world surrounding the project and the abstract world constructed through the models introduced by the methodologies. Such a gap provides an extremely fertile ground for so-called unexpected consequences to flourish.
- *Ideological drift*: projects are sold as utopian promises. Methods are kept alive by ideological discourses to defend positions and seek legitimacy. Preaching encapsulates science. Painful and slow alignment of people, methods, and systems is the stuff of which actual implementation processes are made.

The phenomenon we want to come closer to generates both the (false) appearances and the apparitions (the actual symptoms), but itself usually remains hidden. A way to unveil it is to start from what has been carefully left out of current approaches to systems design and management by both the managers and the participants. We refer here to human existence, the designers' and users' practical dealings in the life world of systems in development and systems in use. In particular, their concerns as human beings facing uncertainty being thrown into situations; the intertwining between their personal trajectories and the project execution; their identities as subjects; and the unavoidable openness of any project or innovation, which rarely fails to resonate with the existential openness of the participants' own life projects. Indeed, the successful completion of any initiative may well depend upon the marrying up of the existential traits with the objectivized characteristics of the project.

In general, one cannot separate human life as a whole from what one can achieve during an innovation, the launch of a project, or a new development. Although such initiatives are all future oriented, and the accompanying methodologies put exclusive emphasis on the management and execution of the *in-order-to*s of the project (see Chapter 8), they inevitably share a lot with the participants' experience and personal history. The in-order-to injunctions are supposed to mobilize the attention and resources of the project members towards a future state of affairs, but it is the members' biographical, historical, and ethical *because-of* motives which can endow the innovation or the project with meaning and momentum.

If the project, goals, and plans do not make sense to those called on to implement them, only perfunctory or distracted compliance will follow. To disregard the complex chemistry and balance between the because-of and in-order-to motives of action may lead to many of the unexpected consequences for both successful and failed innovations. But such an existential balance is extremely precarious, if not contradictory. On the one hand, any development is supposed to lead along a carefully planned trajectory to a better future state. Any deviation can be controlled and the course restored or improved by feedback and learning. Thus, it is an endeavour full of rational promises laid out in front of the actor by the structured methodologies. On the other hand, the personal past experience and trajectory remain blurred, and the actor has to cope with the fact of being *thrown* into the project or use situation almost by chance, or by a series of circumstances largely outside her control. Furthermore, her past, made up of cognitive frames and scripts, can hamper her ability to learn, in ways she is hardly aware of. As a result, any development will result in an inextricable mix of failure and success, with many minor or major unintended consequences which can trigger new learning and innovations, or just lead to frustrating vicious circles. The sense of achievement and discovery will always be intertwined with the anxiety of failure, falling, and drifting. Alas, none of these preoccupations, which are closer to our existence, gets featured in the countless methodologies developed by the software engineering institutes all over the industrialized world.

An ambiguous stranger

Hospitality was first deployed as a promising candidate notion to interpret the surprising evolution of a groupware system in a large European consumer goods company (see the Unilever case mentioned in Chapter 5). The case dealt with a fairly large application of Lotus Notes coupled with a worldwide team-based organization for new product development. Dedicated Notes applications were built to allow multidisciplinary and multinational teams to work jointly on common projects, regardless of the distance between locations. Implementation of the new system was carried out according to a participative methodology, an incremental introduction, and comprehensive training. Usage was immediate, ubiquitous, and successful. One day, however, a cheering message broadcast over the network by a top marketing manager in London made every user realize that the new transparent platform could be deployed by headquarters as a powerful controlling eye, able to access any working document or the local bulletin board of any distant team. Usage fell immediately and significantly. Attempts to revamp the system succeeded only when the applications were redesigned to replicate the pre-existing routines and organizational structures, thus losing much of the original innovative design, transparency, and collaboration opportunities.

This case provides evidence, among other things, about the ambiguity of new technology: despite the careful planning and design and the extensive training, new technology appears to the user suddenly as an ambivalent, threatening stranger. The latent tensions between the professional dimension and the existential one exploded as a consequence of a small incident: underlying anxieties about the new ways of working and the new powerful tool could not be tamed even by an advanced design concept and a careful project management plan.

Hospitality describes the phenomenon of dealing with new technology as an ambiguous stranger. Hospitality is a human institution: it is about being receptive and adopting; managing boundaries between what or who is known, and what or who is unknown. Hospitality is a first step in accepting the Other. It deals with that moment of truth, already recognized by marketing experts during the routinized, but still fatal (for the customer's experience of the airline service), check-in procedure in airports. It is a singularity, a catastrophe point, when the real world is hit and what it means to be human is put to the test. This existential knot is carefully avoided by methodologies too abstract and high-flying to deal with such a human and worldly moment, lest they risk being caught by surprise when such events and forces creep in and burst out unexpectedly, and sudden apparitions, coming from nowhere, disrupt irreversibly the carefully crafted appearances of rationality, planning, and control.

Is hospitality the hidden phenomenon that generates both the false appearances of systems development methodologies and the array of symptoms that point to the fact that such methodologies ultimately play a limited role in actual system development, despite their claims, buttressed by appeals to superior management knowledge, to the contrary?

A tentative answer may come from the following enquiry into what hospitality is.

Multiple worlds in a word

The dictionary of the Indo-European institutions dedicates to 'hospitality' a short, but dense section. It is a word that has multiple, twisted, and even conflicting origins and meanings (Benveniste 1969). In Latin, host is *hospes, hostipets,* and *hostis.* The last word, however, means also enemy, thus revealing that ambiguity between friend and enemy which underlies the phenomenon of hospitality. In Latin, words which include *potis* refer to power, owner, *despot* and *potest* (to be able to). These can be linked to earlier words meaning 'one's own' and 'belonging to'. *Potis* is, then, linked to *ipse* (same) and in general to the identity of the subject.

Hostis (corresponding to the Gothic *gast*) is guest (favourable stranger) and enemy (hostile guest). Originally, *hostes* were those foreigners who had equal citizen rights to the Romans. In a related sense, the verb *hostire* meant to be equivalent to, equate. *Hostis* reveals, then, a bundle of commitments such as reciprocity, equal exchange, balance, and compensation. With the establishment of more stable boundaries defining Roman citizenship, the institution of 'foreigners treated equally' disappears, and *hostis* refers only to an enemy, while host becomes *hospes*; or *hostipets*, the lord of the house who welcomes the Other (a similar interplay of words happens in modern English, between host and hostile).

We leave the etymological analysis at this point, having retained the following suggestions. Hospitality is indeed a catastrophic point in social relations: it can turn into hostility. Hospitality has to do with identity, that of the lord-subject and the foreign visitor, since identity gets defined through alterity. As an institution it includes a nexus of commitments, from reciprocity to fair exchange and compensation.

The organization as a host: a matter of identity

Effective hospitality creates a (partial and temporary) symmetry between the host/subject/lord/owner and the (weaker) guest. This is achieved by introducing a new asymmetry and adopting culturally dependent rituals by which the host becomes the server of the guest. The latter can behave as if she were in her own home.

The importance of certain values within the hosting organization can capsize. For example, in studying the different degrees of hospitality exhibited by two French rugby teams, one with an established tradition and culture, the other with less of both, Darbon (1997) discovers that the 'Great Rugby Family' can show quite different degrees of openness towards the outsider. High internal solidarity, if accompanied by a strong culture and long tradition, seems to make the team less permeable to the newcomer, while, paradoxically, weaker cultures may be more willing to extend their internal network of solidarity to include the outsider. This study raises doubts about the unexpected side effects of those heavy investments recommended by the current management literature, aspiring at the establishment of a robust corporate culture, especially when the aim is to be able to host the new nomadic hordes and technologies. On the other hand, hospitality has an advantage: her act of reaching out while expressing hospitality through various forms of commitments helps the host's (partially) new identity to emerge. This echoes the Maussian argument by which identity results from the network of exchanges and relationships with others.

Hospitality is about crossing a boundary, reaching out to the Other, the Stranger, though without abolishing such a boundary. The host must deal with the ambiguity of the Stranger, who can be a friend or an enemy. If hosting is about weakening one's own identity to enrich it, reaching out to the Other means establishing the new symmetry: recognizing and accepting the identity of the Other, at least on a temporary basis. Hospitality is the human process of making the Other a human like oneself. Hosting the new technology means, then, accepting a paramount symmetry between humans and non-humans.

In particular, consider systems development as a process by which the organization hosts the technology. The perspective of hospitality reveals a number of surprising features of this process, which is usually looked at as a structured technical activity or as a political struggle:

- being able to host the technology will redefine our identities;
- unexpected consequences only signal that any attempt to control the technology fully is doomed to failure: hospitality involves at best intelligent servicing of the new technology;
- different cultures prescribe different codes, norms, and rituals for hospitality: the guest has to accept them. In the case of system development conceived as hosting the new technology, methodologies constitute today's rituals imposed by humans on the technology;
- following Kant's (1972) discussion of the universal right to hospitality, humans should grant a set of rights to technology such as the right to visit, but not necessarily the right to stay—it is not only human guests that are condemned to be nomadic, technologies should be able to wander, too—recall also the idea of being able 'to say yes and no' to modern technology put forward by Heidegger (see Chapter 4), or the injunction by Weick (1993) to 'be able to drop our tools!' in an emergency.
- if the guest is perceived as hostile, the host will treat him as an enemy (recall the Luddites).

Technology as a guest: the influence of the stranger

In a first instance technology, as a guest, presents itself to the host as endowed with affordances. Affordances trigger a network of commitments by the host: they define the contours of her role as designer, sponsor, or user (see Chapter 5). But that is just the beginning of an open-ended process: the guest also possesses its own dynamics and will begin to align the host according to certain needs and constraints. Note how hospitality diverges from straightforward command and control as pre-scribed by structured methodologies: in order to remain the master of the house, the host must instead release control and serve the guest. Service is in the first instance compliance with affordances.

Consequences for the guest-technology are then:

- through hospitality technology is made human: the human-ization of systems can be a more intriguing challenge than the virtualization of reality;
- technology can consider the hosting organization, as it were, at its own service, but it cannot dominate it;
- when technology turns into an enemy, it will exploit the organization and its members, finding allies among certain groups in the organization, but at the same time dropping them when it no longer needs them. The studies of infra-structure, as reported in Chapter 5, show precisely this point.

Connecting two separate worlds

Hospitality connects the inside (the home) with the outside (the visitor). It links the settler with the visiting, mobile guest. Hospitality is about managing the threshold, in the real and

figurative sense (the edge of the catastrophe in human relationships between friend and enemy). Hospitality leads to innovation and learning, because it requires a cognitive displacement in
a foreign territory and culture, but without travelling: it is a sort
of stationary nomadism. When the two cultures are too far
apart, the role of mediators in facilitating hospitality can be
crucial. In any case, hospitality involves the risk of misunder-
standing, since it typically has to deal with communication
across different languages and cultural modes. The guest is
intrinsically ambiguous, and can turn into an enemy. Both can
become hostages of each other. It is thus a relationship that has
to be based on trust, although a trust that cannot be cultivated
within the boundaries of a clan only, but between separate clans.
If the host becomes a guest in his own home, then the guest
becomes a sort of host: thus, technology hosts the humans
thanks to its own array of affordances. Systems development
becomes the intriguing business for humans to find ways of
being hosted by the technology (we can recall Kubrick's movie
2001 where the astronauts slowly discover that they are HAL's,
the spaceship computer's, powerless guests). Standards, the
installed base, infrastructures, languages, and interfaces can be
now looked at as the rituals imposed on humans as guests by the
ICT infrastructure.

In sum, hospitality, seen as the main phenomenon of the
encounter between technology and organizations, shows that
systems development methodologies are just the external
appearance of a ritual imposed by the human host. They may be
carefully planned but cannot dispose of the unpredictability and
ambiguity of the guest. Understanding hospitality as a phenomenon we have to deal with when designing, implementing, and
using new technologies is not a purely intellectual exercise.
Through such an understanding we can escape the programme

and priorities set by the rituals of methodologies, and be ready to explore new ways of rearranging our commitments towards ourselves as designers and users, and towards the technology as a non-human, ambiguous guest. A different agenda can be thus set out in dealing with new technologies. Trust and friendliness must be coupled with a releasement of control (recall: the host must play the server). Acceptance of the guest's intrinsic ambiguity and mystery, what Ciborra and Lanzara (1994) have called, borrowing the expression from the poet Keats, 'negative capability', should become part of the practical ways of coping with technology. To be sure, an effective host must be able to exercise various forms of care depending upon the unpredictable circumstances in the unfolding of hospitality. Finally, host and guest will most probably be engaged in forms of reciprocal cultivation by sharing and enriching their respective cultures and practices.

Thinking, behaving, and acting in terms of hospitality should improve our encounters with technology and unleash those energies we usually invest in the straitjacket of methods. The ubiquity of processes like *bricolage*, tinkering, and improvisation in the design of organizations and the use of complex technical systems, despite the massive pressure to adopt and deploy rational methodologies, can then be appreciated in a different light. These highly situated human activities are far from being the result of the practitioner as an artist, or a snob. They belong to the core of the human institution of hospitality. They express the many subtle ways in which we ingeniously discover, discern, interpret, and act upon the shades of our encounter with new technology as an ambiguous stranger.

To conclude, the notion of hospitality introduces a universe of discourse closer to human existence and its basic institutions, able to grant an existential indexing to systems development activities, while avoiding those too readily accepted functional role definitions, such as human factors. Thinking, acting, and behaving in terms of hospitality allow something more constructive: the re-registering of our networks of dues and commitments to a strange actant (the technology) around a strange attractor, the multifaceted and catastrophic point of encounter (see Table 6.1).

A last comment is apposite regarding the broader social context in which hospitality towards technology is taking place. If the nomadic society of the future will be a market society, as repeatedly asserted by various scholars of transaction costs economics, what is the role of hospitality in a market society? Are these two institutions (hosting and trading) compatible? To be sure, they are closer than it would appear at first. We can turn back to where we started this chapter. Etymology indicates that hospitality has to do not only with reciprocity (for example, gifts) but also, more economically speaking, with the measurement of equality in transactions and fairness in exchange. Once again, the dictionary of the Indo-European languages, ranging from Latin to Iranian, would show the multiple and surprising links between words such as: friend, contract, exchange, reciprocity, and guest. In Iranian mythology the god of hospitality is called Aryaman. *Arya* is a word denoting people belonging to the same linguistic community. Aryaman is the mediator who allows newcomers to become members of the clan, through marriage, contract, and exchange. In modern Iranian *aryaman* is the intimate friend. The closely associated word *erman* means guest.

Table 6.1. *The old and new commitments in systems development and hospitality*

The old commitments (as dictated by systems development methodologies)	The new commitments (dictated by hospitality)
Strong identity and advocacy	Define identity in a plastic way depending upon the guest(s)
Enforce boundaries, standards, roles	Cross boundaries, test standards and roles
Be rational	Care
Seek consensus	Be the server of
Be in control of the tool	Release control
Measure	Listen
Compare, learn, and improve	Share
Be in control of unexpected consequences	Be open to mysteries and ambiguities (negative capability)

7

Shih

Try for a moment to put into brackets your current efforts at restructuring or streamlining your organization, or for that matter, at creating your brand new e-business. You may be engaged in process re-engineering, customer reorientation, or e-commerce. Try to abstract yourself from all that and reflect on what is fundamental in what you are doing while engaged in business transformation or creation. You do not want to hold to a specific methodology, or the latest managerial model: you have tried out so many in the past, and you know you will be obliged to do the same in the future, probably at an even faster rate. Thus, what is fundamental cannot be the methodologies or the models, past and future. What is fundamental is the trying out itself, the relentless experimenting and not the specific, contingent approach being implemented at a given moment in time.

This chapter was originally published as C. U. Ciborra (1996), 'The platform organization: recombining strategies, structures and surprises', *Organization Science*, 7/2 (Mar.–Apr.): 103–18.

Forget, then, process as an object you design or re-engineer according to the latest methodology. Rather, consider and dwell on your daily business of existence at work: a process of unceasingly recombining resources. Such recombination is the main activity around which competing and organizing revolve. Indeed, at the heart of economic development is our ability to play with a virtually limitless set of possibilities in order to find ever better ways of doing things. Such notions as the interchangeability of product parts and of organizational activities, as well as the capacity to try out new combinations of resources continuously, are what generates economic growth.

It was the radical shifts in the organization of work, from the factory system, to mass production, to flexible manufacturing, that led to dramatic leaps in productivity. Modern forms of economic organization, such as alliances or networked and federated firms, are considered to be at the forefront in terms of combinations of routines and transactions which can deliver higher efficiency. However, one should not ignore that uncertainty is an equally important issue in determining the particular efficient configuration of resources emerging at a given point in time, as well as the speed and frequency at which recombinations take place. On the one hand, the birth rate of new organizational forms that populate the industrial landscape can be measured in decades, if not half-centuries. On the other, the current pace of competition and technological development requires a much quicker generation (and elimination) of new arrangements, at least in the high-tech industries. In a rapidly changing environment none of the well-known organizational arrangements may optimize resource utilization. We submit that, at best, one can only settle for a shapeless organization that keeps generating new forms through frequent recombination. Using a by now historic case of a high-tech firm, we put forward a model of *the platform*: a chameleon-like organization conceived as a laboratory for rapid restructuring. The platform turns out to be an unrecognized source of productivity in the high-tech industries, because of its intrinsic potential to generate efficiently new combinations of resources, routines, and structures which are able to match turbulent market circumstances.

From the structural point of view the platform is the resilient outcome manufactured out of the ingenious reconciliation of existing organizational mechanisms and forms, picked by management according to subjective and situated plans and interpretations (see Chapters 3 and 8). Its most distinctive attributes are its flexibility, movement, and transformability arising from the intersecting, penetrating, and collating of different organizational arrangements, such as the network, the matrix, and even the hierarchy. It is simultaneously fragmented and intertwined, and thus may be the only form capable of surviving in a high-tech industry where a monolithic, rigid business identity is not able to cope with the frantic pace of technological change. In contrast to any traditional (static) form, we have here the celebration of all the qualities of the random, the apparently incidental, the seemingly oppositional, as well as the surprising. Analogous to the concept of building-as-landscape in deconstructivist architecture, the platform emerges as an exciting mixture of ready-made arrangements and interpretations, and of half-realized, incomplete solutions and visions.

In the mind of its members the platform works as a collective cognitive engine enacted by a pool of flexible human resources for exploring and trying out multiple combinations of old and new organizational arrangements. The platform is a model which turns upside down our beliefs about what is structural and permanent in the strategy–structure dyad, as well as what is subjective, informal, and ephemeral. It does so simply because its job is of a particular nature: to handle frequent, sudden, and radical changes, not just in products, markets, and technologies, but in the very business identity and industries to which it belongs at that moment in time. Specifically, its purpose is to support managers facing frequent surprises: events which appear to be incomprehensible or inconceivable, as they represent fundamental disjunctures, where existing frames, assumptions, and values fall apart, and organizational problem solving and the design of ad-hoc initiatives lack a meaningful context (see the next chapter).

The platform is powerful because it embeds the potential for action. It seeks out the intrinsic dispositions of resources so that they can be recombined when needed more quickly and effectively (Jullien 1995). In the platform strategy, action and structure coalesce as an entity designed for coping with surprises. Such a potential corresponds to the Chinese concept of *shih*, which we can trace in Sun-Tzu's (1993) classic treatise on war. Waging a war effectively relies, according to the Chinese strategist, on the exploitation of the contours (configuration) of the resources at hand. *Shih*, then, captures the strategic disposition for action of things organizational.

Snapshots from a significant period (1977–1990)

Our case is Olivetti, at the time of the study a leading European computer vendor that underwent innumerable organizational changes and became one of the first examples of a network corporation. Olivetti represents an exciting setting for exploring how a strategy-in-action unfolds. Its unique management style gave rise to policies and strategies which were often called into question or criticized. The Italian multinational was regarded as an 'unpredictable giant', one that did not belong to the same league as the US and Japanese manufacturers who dominated the computer industry at that time. While the big boys understood each other, they could not quite fathom or anticipate the strategic moves of their smaller competitor.

In 1989 Olivetti ranked ninth among the top world computer manufacturers. It had been sixth at the beginning of the decade, eighth in 1982, and it managed to survive during a period of great technological change and industry shake-ups. In Europe, it trailed IBM and jockeyed with Siemens and Bull for second place. Though strongly rooted in Italy, less than 40 per cent of its turnover was sold on the home market, making Olivetti the most international of the European computer manufacturers. The number of employees fell from 70,000 in 1976 to 47,000 in 1984, but rose to 57,000 in 1989 following the acquisition of Triumph-Adler (a German office equipment vendor). Returns on revenue had been increasing until the second half of the 1980s, before starting to decline. Note that at the beginning of the 1970s Olivetti was *not* a computer manufacturer: 80 per cent of its sales were of mechanical and electrical calculators, typewriters, and office supplies, including furniture, but by 1977, computer equipment had come to represent 43 per cent of sales and in 1982 it reached 71 per cent. In 1984 Olivetti launched its first MS DOS based personal computer and became, for a couple of years, the world's second-largest producer of PCs. Thus, towards the end of the 1980s, computer products had become a steady 84 per cent of all sales. Since the 1970s the Italian company had crossed at least two technological discontinuities: from mechanics to electronics in its traditional products, typewriters and calculators, and from electronics to microprocessor-based personal computers and workstations. Corresponding and radical changes took place in the organization of work, from the mechanical assembly lines to work groups, to the adoption of highly sophisticated factory automation. The composition of the workforce changed at all levels. For example, in the 1970s researchers were mainly mechanical engineers, while later they became, almost exclusively, software specialists.

What was Olivetti in the early 1990s? An investment report described it as a huge distribution company constantly in search of new products, through both its own R&D and external routes. Once found, it then sold these products through the various distribution channels that it either developed internally or acquired. (A decade later, after a period of crisis and disinvestment from the PC business, Olivetti would buy Telecom Italia, become a telecom company, and continue to transform itself. Those events lie outside the period of this case study. However, the following history should help identify the DNA of such a chameleonic organization.)

Devising and implementing a global technology strategy

In systematic comparisons carried out at the time and aimed at determining the correlation between the R&D intensity of firms in various industries (measured in terms of firms' own R&D spending as a percentage of sales revenues) and worldwide corporate sales growth and company gains in world market share, Olivetti stood out in the computer industry for spending relatively less than competitors such as Digital and Bull, but possessing an above average growth. Correspondingly, the task for the Italian multinational in defining its global technology strategy could be identified as follows: what is the combination of moves and technology acquisitions needed to bolster what otherwise would be a weakness in product breadth and technology, in order that its aggressive distribution channels may be constantly replenished with competitive products and services? A boundary condition, not to be underestimated, for the resolution of such a problem is the management of the dramatic changes required to transform and adjust the internal organization (skills, workforce size, work organization, R&D, production processes, management and marketing cultures) each time a new technology is adopted. Despite its moderate economic performance, Olivetti's number of successful attempts at managing such a technology strategy was judged as one of the highest in the world, and a key to its longer-term survival. When juggling to enact its global technology strategy through alliances, Olivetti was a pioneer: more robust companies at the time, like Digital, IBM, or Apple, would learn to face similar problems just a decade later, not always successfully.

To the outside observer, Olivetti's technology strategy-in-action presented two faces over the period considered. First, in the articulated mix of moves deployed to give substance to opportunistic technology acquisitions strategy one recognizes the wisdom that Olivetti's management presented to the outside world. Its darker side was the idiosyncratic and unique style of management, which baffled competitors and allies alike when dealing with the Italian company. Indeed, we might find it difficult to follow the logic of the continuous changes in structures, the debilitating see-saw of hopes, failures, and unexpected successes of many strategic moves (especially the alliances), and the sudden shifts in conduct that seem more the result of a day-to-day myopic search than the outcome of the grandiose plans evoked whenever a new global move was announced.

Top internal sources conceded that the technology strategy mostly developed in an *implicit* way during the period that led from typewriters to personal computers. Take, for example, the PC. Initially, Olivetti was a minor player, in terms not only of volume, but also of R&D. For one thing, its location was distant from the loci of crucial innovations in hardware, software, and systems. Also, the overall thrust remained unclear. Indeed, when a company is only a minor player in the computer industry, there is the temptation to try to rapidly become a global competitor, and thus to spread R&D resources over many projects, but this tends to dilute efforts, as many European computer manufacturers came to realize in the 1970s. The implicit, emerging strategy was to focus instead on only some areas of strength, such as distributed data processing, abandoning the mainframe business in a much-debated disinvestment. In such areas a series of interventions were carried out to support internal R&D. The strategic choice made depended upon circumstances. It could have been the acquisition of a company that had a low market value, but which gave access to a niche in an important country, as in the case of Acorn computers in the UK; or a joint venture with a technologically more advanced competitor in order to revamp a product line and rescue what was left of an internal design team, as in the case of OCI, a successful joint venture with Canon Italy, in the photocopying business.

Strategy managers mentioned two factors that accounted for this inner logic:

1. The product life cycle (from emerging technologies to mature products):
    • global alliances were often forged in order to secure growth by gaining access to new markets, capital, new technologies, and joint product development;

- joint R&D with key suppliers (e.g. Intel, Microsoft) was pursued to tap sources of innovation for future products, the development of which fell largely outside the control of Olivetti this implied placing bets on who the key suppliers would be during the next round of innovation;
- pre-competitive research, for example through publicly (EU) funded projects, was aimed at collecting resources for basic research and new applications;
- venture capital was used to identify opportunities and access new technological developments in a focused way;
- joint ventures were set up to revamp old businesses or re-enter markets previously abandoned; and finally,
- acquisitions were pursued to gain market share in established businesses and mature products.

2. Product complexity and the company's relative strength:
   - joint ventures were sought for surviving alongside technology leaders;
   - venture capital was deployed in order to gain access to specific, sophisticated technologies;
   - less complex products may simply have required an increased market share through acquisitions.

The global technology strategy was enacted through a number of organizational units within the company. The Strategy Department was mainly responsible for the definition and launch of the technology strategy, and coordinated the activities related to their implementation. Within its boundaries separate units dealt with each of the strategic directions identified above. The Strategy Department had its own corporate R&D unit, which enlarged and shrank many times over the period studied. The variety of lines along which the technology strategy was developed over time and the shifting definition of the supporting organizational structures point to the complexity of the process. But do not be deceived: the neat systematization and rationalization that Olivetti top managers provided during seminars and interviews should not conceal the pragmatic nature of the entire process and its inherent uncertainty, nor should the role that surprises played during implementation be underestimated.

Identity building across discontinuities

In general, then, top management at Olivetti linked, at least *ex post facto*, their global technology strategy to the product life cycle, or better, to the various generations of products that were put on the market. However, two conflicting accounts must be reconciled: on the one hand management pointed to an approach whereby strategic responses were deployed to meet a set of technological changes; on the other, they admitted that no implementation plan could match the actual sequence of actions: improvisation predominated over strategic planning. How are we to reconcile such opposing views?

To begin with, recall that Olivetti had been constantly dealing with successive life cycles of technologies rather than mere generations of products, to the extent that the company originally assembled mechanical and then electrical typewriters; then electromechanical systems, electronic typewriters; followed by PCs and minicomputers; and, later in the period, considered generic computer platforms. During each period, when one technology was clearly prevailing over the others, management had a more focused product life cycle approach in setting a technology strategy. However, in order to implement such policies, Olivetti management needed an identity: first as a firm operating in the mechanical industry; then as an office equipment vendor which sold a variety of office systems and products ranging from typewriters to photocopiers; then as a computer manufacturer which sold PCs and minicomputers; and later as a system integrator operating predominantly in the software industry. The key issue during each phase of technology was to build an identity (culture, mission, market position, design skills, customers, suppliers, etc.) as a major player in that industry. Once such an identity was acquired, the management of the life cycle of specific products would follow suit. During each stage, having an identity was an important matter, as lacking one could severely hamper managerial action, even when good knowledge of the market and the technology was available. Entering into a new industry makes you feel marginal, and, in lacking self-confidence, you may be excessively tentative in trying out new policies and products. This becomes less and less the case as the new identity builds up, although other problems may emerge, such as arrogance, sometimes accompanied by bureaucratization, which works to stifle flexibility and the capacity for effective response to new situations. Of course, this has always been the case for firms in industries that have gradually changed their product range or initiated a diversification strategy. The distinctive aspect, however, for Olivetti, and other companies such as NCR, already operating in the computer industry and sharing similar histories, is that the technology—as distinct from the product—life cycle was extremely short and became increasingly shorter. Thus, these companies must migrate from one industry to another, and even create new ones, at a pace that would have been frantic even for the simple implementation of product changes within a stable technological horizon. The most frustrating implication of this identity building process is that a new identity must be trashed when one would like to keep it, when, after a painful learning process, one has become not just a pioneer, but a leader. On several occasions, Olivetti had to give up the idea of being a pioneer (as in the case of mainframes, during the second half of the 1960s, or in the multimedia workstations during the study period), but this did not exempt the company from the necessity of implementing radical changes, given the closely succeeding shifts of technological paradigms. For example, Olivetti reached a very high level of perfection in mechanical comptometers (their performance could compete with the early electronic calculators), precisely when it was time to abandon that technology to embark on the more uncertain job of assembling electronic systems. Similarly, when proficient in VDUs and minis, it had to try out the PC, and when it came out with one of the first on the market, the M20, Olivetti had to discontinue its production, because IBM was fast imposing the MS DOS standard. At each discontinuity the competencies acquired in a given field became, in part, useless, given the competence-destroying character of most innovations.

In such a perspective, the problem of defining the mission and direction of R&D, and, in general terms, the global technology strategy, does not consist of choosing an alternative among various product lines or markets, but, more radically, of repeatedly asking the question, 'what business are we in?': it is the identity of the product, the market, the production process, and the boundaries between what should be done internally and what has to be procured externally, knowing that many of the core innovations are in the hands of external suppliers?

The subjectivity factor should not be overlooked, either. Though the technology strategy could be seen as the outcome of objective forces, such as market pull and technology push during a given technological stage, the subjective, interpretative element represented by management perception is what shapes the ultimate thrust to action. Even for a given product technology, the strategist has difficulties in finding objective features on which to develop a plan for action. For example, at the end of the 1980s one could consider the PC as a product being pulled by the market. And indeed the PC could be looked at just as a commodity, a box, for which vendors should acquiesce to low margins and, if anything, scramble to find new means to increase market share and production volumes. But another perspective can be envisaged: one of the PC as an engineering workstation in miniature. According to the latter perspective, management should turn their attention to the core of workstation technology chips and their architecture, present and future. What will the emerging standard for platforms be? Does a platform standard need to be pushed on the market, through the chips of the existing high-end machines? The answer cannot be found just by looking at the apparently objective characteristics of the product and the market. Both are highly plastic, if not purely subjective, much like the identity of a firm operating in the high-tech industries. No matter how the organization's management is set up to address their existential problem, it is bound to be revisable and ephemeral. As a consequence, the search for an identity across a technological or business discontinuity requires determination and commitment, quickness and passion, wisdom and detachment. In such a fluid industry, extreme confidence, caution, or attachment may hinder curiosity and openness, while an attitude tolerant of knowledge and ignorance may improve adaptability.

The organizational structures supporting the technology strategy must be able to cope simultaneously with the management of discontinuities and of incremental innovation. This has put, over time, a premium on the firm's ability to develop multiple, often inconsistent competencies, so as to deal with the emerging, divergent technological and organizational requirements. As a result, existing structures, procedures, and frames, which influence action, are usually under severe strain, and managers end up feeling they are operating in a very fuzzy organizational environment. For instance, even if structures are in place to guide behaviour and there is an effort to revise them radically each year, everyone knows that they are only marginally relevant at the moment of action, and what matters is the possibility that one has of relying on a personal network of colleagues located in the various units of the organization. Thus, while functional departments came and went, and might well have represented formal changes in authority and communication, still decision making occurred through a set of arrangements (network, hierarchy or clan, or a mixture thereof) which evolved according to a logic difficult to capture, for no written record was, or could be, available and no formal memo sanctioned the actual changes. Only crucial events, and the related narratives forming the background memory of the organization, provided insiders with a record of the evolution of such latent structures. As an example we can look at the formal shifts in the organization of the corporate R&D unit, to whom the unit reports, its management, and its direction, and the relatively little impact they seemed to have on the company's conduct.

- The changes in the assignments, responsibilities, and mission of the unit were radical, but also temporary.
- Some aspects that were fuzzy, like the unit's mission-in-practice and its relationship with the rest of the organization, probably continued to stay fuzzy. Everyone relied mainly on individual personalities to let the unit drift in a direction believed to be the most suitable; the rest of the organization knew it, and top management knew that the rest of the organization knew; hence, who needed to be officially informed?

• Actual decision making frequently involved the previous
  network of people and everybody seemed to be aware of it;
  this further confirms that formal modifications were marginal, and that in practice changes emerged from surprises
  along the extant drifting route, or continued to be enforced
  by the old boys' network.

To conclude, the degree of complexity in operating in the IT
industry not only affects the nature of the primary task to be
accomplished, but the very identity of the business. Coping with
identity uncertainty requires responses that are at least one order
of magnitude higher than dealing with task uncertainty alone.
However, such a distinction may blur during action, when
events and circumstances present themselves as a mélange difficult to disentangle, and actors cope with them by retrieving
established models, but then discarding these models pragmat-
ically. Though managers picture themselves as being busy in
decision making (forecasting, planning, and selecting alternative
courses of action) according to the standard strategy models,
they would be better described as engaged in 'sensemaking'
(Weick 1979), relentlessly picking up the pieces and leftovers of
the superseded cosmologies (past plans, marketing choices,
goals, and outlooks) and trying to paste them together in order
to make new sense of the emerging technologies, markets, and
industries they are enacting. The rapid succession of identities
puts strain on the strategy–structure link and, as a result, formal
structures appear to be continuously revised, fragmented, and
trumped up. However, an underlying continuity was maintained
(for example, the top management group was relatively homo-
geneous and stable throughout this period): therefore there must be
a hidden context that kept providing sense to managerial action.
In order to unveil such an underlying context, it is illuminating

to analyse how Olivetti coped with major breakdowns, or surprises, when implementing its technology strategy during this period.

Alliances, acquisitions, and surprises

The ability to implement a global technology strategy by setting up alliances of various sorts and exploiting them more for their unexpected outcomes than for their original goals became one of Olivetti's core competencies: a capability that other computer companies also ended up following when they eventually had to face discontinuities in their businesses. Partnerships were sought for two main reasons: access to capital and access to know-how in order to achieve rapid growth. Growth was needed to survive during the continuing computer industry shake-out, when a rather fragmented industry structure gave way to an oligopoly of a few remaining major players. In that scenario, Olivetti tried to become a global competitor, in terms of sales volume, geographic scope of operations, and product range. Internal growth would have been the preferred alternative, but the required speed of transformation was so high compared to the resources available that alliances were sought instead. The economics of growth and change are characterized by many unexpected, paradoxical manifestations and Schumpeter (1950) remains unsurpassed in qualifying it as a process of 'creative destruction'.

As a first example, take the strategic alliance with AT&T, the main one that Olivetti was involved with during the period considered. Established in 1983, it was a highly asymmetric partnership given the size of the companies (AT&T was roughly ten times as large as Olivetti); type of core technology (telecoms vs. office equipment); type of culture, history, location, and markets served. Originally the agreement included an equity participation of AT&T equal to about 24 per cent of Olivetti's capital, but it had a broader scope for which the equity participation was supposed to indicate a formal commitment. In general, it is possible to identify the main goals of that alliance as follows:

- 'governing' the competition, by creating a constellation of anti-IBM firms; imposing a new operating system standard (Unix) in Europe; and easing the access of both companies to each other's markets;
- enriching the partners' competencies, such as mastering the convergence between telecommunications and computer technologies;
- transferring complementary managerial skills, for AT&T had public monopoly know-how, while Olivetti was strongly market oriented;
- sharing R&D projects and results; and, perhaps most importantly, the need for the two corporations to become global players both geographically and technologically.

AT&T wanted to transform itself, after the deregulation, into an 'information company', rather than just a telecom operator. Olivetti aimed at overcoming, once and for all, the narrow boundaries of the European market.

The global agreement represented a framework for collaboration in various sectors including R&D; reciprocal sales of each other's products; joint development of new ones; up to the cross-transfer of personnel. AT&T got out of Olivetti in 1989; yet, even before reaching the breakdown point, at which time the two companies gave up the systematic development of a common strategy, the alliance had a bumpy evolution: only a few of its stated goals were attained. However, there were also some positive surprises: for example, Olivetti, as a supplier to AT&T,

almost immediately became a major vendor of PCs to the American market. It also found itself in a good position to develop Unix-based systems with the help of the Bell Labs. AT&T's investment was a success as Olivetti's share value almost quadrupled. The transfer of personnel reached its peak when the director of Olivetti of America went to manage the troubled AT&T Information Systems division.

There were also disappointments on both sides, of course: joint R&D never went beyond Unix, in which AT&T maintained an undisputed leadership; and the delivery of PCs was later discontinued because there were quality problems, and consequently AT&T was not able to sell them in large quantities on the American market. In general, the management of the US firm gradually became wary of wanting to become an information company and retrenched to its core business, to what it knew best, that is, telecommunications and networking.

We should next consider what happened during the daily management of the alliance. Most likely, power games, procedures, and practices to curb opportunism were the stuff that continuous renegotiations of the alliance were made of. But these were relevant only for the mundane aspects of the partnering process. Growth, enhanced cooperation, the capability to establish long-term projects and commitments, the willingness and ability to merge corporate cultures in a constructive way were issues on an agenda that went well beyond daily haggling. The alliance constituted a general framework, a declaration of common intent: but it included some detailed agreements, for example on the development of new products or the formulation of common projects. In the absence of such detailed agreements, the alliance could still work very smoothly: it could be a satisfactory investment, involving equity acquisitions, or satisfying subcontracting requirements, which might even deliver lower transaction costs compared to the market. Nonetheless it was a failure, since it did not allow one or both partners to reach their stated goals of rapid growth and diversification.

In other words, efficient alliances may be ineffective or meaningless. In retrospect, this may have been the major flaw in the Olivetti–AT&T strategic partnership. The collapse of the alliance was not due to fears of being robbed by the opportunistic partner, but rather due to the lack of appropriate learning skills for exploiting the alliance as a new resource. Thus, organizational inertia rather than preoccupation with patents turned out to be a critical failure factor.

In this respect, the successful acquisition of Acorn can be compared with the problematic relationship with AT&T's Bell Laboratories. In the former case, while preserving the autonomy of Acorn, top researchers from the smaller and more innovative British firm were transferred to Olivetti's R&D unit, among them its director, who revolutionized the unit. New products based on RISC technology introduced from the British company were jointly developed, and a new direction of research into multimedia workstations was established. In accordance with Olivetti's partnering policies Acorn had been originally acquired to gain market share in the UK and a strong foothold in the education market. After the acquisition both of these objectives lost their significance because of the dire financial situation of the company. However, it came as a surprise that Acorn's labs contained a wealth of people, skills, and continuing projects that turned out to be of strategic relevance, putting Olivetti on a new track. More precisely, they enabled Olivetti to pursue the option to be a leader in workstation technology instead of being just a follower of IBM. Under Acorn's director, and for a period of five years, R&D emphasized an autonomous development activity in multimedia workstations, by experimenting with and examining through prototypes and exploratory products the features that were to be included in the next generation of portable office systems. The R&D unit was restructured as a network of laboratories, each developing specific functionalities of an advanced workstation: image and speech recognition, multimedia, artificial intelligence, etc. A computer network connected the laboratories situated in Italy, California, England, and Germany, and nearby research, university, and industrial innovation centres. To be sure, all this did not happen automatically, but was the result of circumstances, together with the capability of Olivetti's vice president for strategy to notice the weak signals that the small, financially troubled British company was sending out. He was able to interpret them and value the invisible assets existing there by taking the bold move of having a foreign scientist of the newly acquired company head corporate R&D. There was a further implication: at the time R&D reported to and advised the Strategy Department, so the new ideas brought in by Acorn's researchers directly reached the place where global and sector technology and partnering strategies were conceived and implemented.

Olivetti through its different partnering moves towards AT&T and Acorn obtained two important results, though in serendipitous ways: first, to be part of the grouping that set the standards in the PC and minicomputer market (the relationship with AT&T greatly simplified the choice to adopt Unix as a new operating system for the minis); second, to accelerate internal learning and absorption of new knowledge through a marked de-provincialization of management.

For almost any alliance the elements of surprise and *bricolage* seem to play a role at least as important as the specific contractual arrangements adopted. Sometimes, as in the Acorn case, an acquisition is carried out to appropriate market share and standardized assets that turn out to be volatile, or simply not there; invisible assets are discovered subsequently and appropriated instead. The specific contractual form that allowed the transfer of skills and know-how, far from being selected instrumentally, happened to be there. In the AT&T case the global agreement paved the way to a pure supply transaction, the sale of PCs to AT&T. When the US company first decided to sell PCs, Olivetti was not even thought of as a potential supplier; it was the existence of the recent alliance that suggested to AT&T that it should procure the boxes from Olivetti instead of from a low-cost manufacturer in the Far East. Nor did Olivetti plan for such a supply contract: the newly designed, automated factory, intended to assemble varying volumes of different PCs flexibly, had to be modified in a hurry and turned into a rigid assembly line producing very large volumes of just one model. Surprises, then, rather than technology strategy, seem to determine structure. Structures happen to be there, or, if not ready at hand, they are the flexible outcome of the artful recombination of what is at hand under the specific circumstances.

What are the qualities of an organizational context that lets such recombinations take place without too much stress? We suggest that such qualities can be found in the structure of Olivetti's products at that time: the computer platforms, as the design of the product often influences the conception of the organization manufacturing it. For example, in Olivetti, when the first electronic and modular typewriters were introduced, job design shifted towards semi-autonomous production units-modules. Because of the way in which the structure of hard mechanical products impacts on the analysis and design of the task and production process, the influence of the dominant product design on the organization tends to stay within operations. In the case of information technology, and its soft, abstract, and systemic artefacts, the influence of the dominant design of a system can spread to encompass the organization as a whole.

The organization as a platform

Two major findings have emerged so far. First, in a case like Olivetti, *ex post* rationalizations do not do justice to the richness, contingency, and unpredictability of managerial action in defining a technology strategy and its implementation. Secondly, one major source of uncertainty in defining a strategy is given by the rapid succession of technological discontinuities, requiring not only the dismantling of assembly lines or product teams, but a deeper transformation of the collation of cognitive frames, cultural views, and structural arrangements linked to the very technology that has to be abandoned. In brief, the shift in technology paradigms, especially when they are, as in this case, competence destroying, requires an exit from the extant formative context which generates the prevailing identity, the design approaches, production organization, and marketing strategies, and the rapid establishment of a new one. However, such a transformation can never be achieved completely; management and the organization do not start from scratch with each new technological generation. The company which today manufactures PCs cannot be considered a greenfield start-up: it carries forward its history as the company that until yesterday used to build typewriters. Since the extant, dominant designs are difficult to dislodge, the prevailing current organizational arrangement is a lashed-together combination, a sedimentation of successive formative contexts, so that the people who sell PCs and minis may be still imprisoned in the typewriter salesman's mindset. Again, specialists who design the new standard platforms may be subtly entangled with the attitude prevailing when proprietary operating systems were being developed. Within the boundaries of such a happenstance combination of frames and organizations, where the old can hardly be distinguished from the new, surprises are bound to appear.

The managerial competence in strongest demand is the ability to respond quickly to and learn from surprises, combined with the artful courage to expose oneself to situations which may trigger knowledge creation, as through the various forms of external linkages that Olivetti management were busily setting up and dismantling during the period considered.

A first consequence is that *flexibility* is the paramount criterion for evaluating Olivetti's organizational arrangements put in place to support its global technology strategy, rather than efficiency of coordination structures, or alignment with the diversification strategy selected. Take, for instance, the sweeping change in organizational structure which was implemented at the end of the 1980s: whereby a holding company was created, and separate companies were set up to sell office products, systems and networks, software and peripherals, segmenting functions like R&D, and, most importantly, the up-to-that-time unified sales organization. The reorganization was an attempt to destroy internal management bottlenecks and improve the response to vertical market needs. At the same time, however, a textbook concern for efficiency would have pointed out that there were overlaps and rivalries between similar departments in the new subsidiary companies, given the basic homogeneity of the underlying technology, the chips and the boxes. What, then, are the implications of that restructuring and the others that preceded and followed it?

An interesting clue can be found in the technological innovation of the *computer platform*: in the period considered, the organization of Olivetti replicated, in some important respects, the design and the functioning of a computer platform. The platform concept influences both product and technology strategies, and it became a formidable trigger for recombination at the firm and industry level. The components of a PC are largely standardized, and the box itself is a component of a heterogeneous computing environment in the user's setting. The platform software includes both a standardized basis for specific applications, and features that make the box, maybe minimally, distinctive, though compatible with many differing computing environments. Thanks to the existence of standards, technologies are developed independently from products: technologies can be bundled into specific products at the last minute as required by the market, or as a response to competitors' moves.

Consider how organizational structures are designed and redesigned. Management pick existing models prescribed by organization theory, consulting advice, and established management practice, or imitate solutions implemented by competitors. These design efforts concern the broad architecture, or configuration, of the formal organization, the one modified by *fiat*, thus always in want of legitimization, provided by the adoption of prevailing management thinking. As far as the real, rather than the formal, organization is concerned, management proceeds in the same magpie fashion. This time, however, the relevant perceptions, imaginations, and solutions are much more subjective, local, and ad hoc: they are carried out under the influence of the extant formative context. In such a culture of practices and visions, the impacts of market forces, new approaches, and solutions are often mediated by the characteristics and functions of the technologies embedded in the product. In a computer firm the design of the technological systems easily becomes a focal point where problem solvers look for the most appropriate solutions. Archetypal technological designs will lurk in the back of their minds when trying to cope with a new challenge, and will appear as a self-evident, familiar, and thus reliable concept, to be employed as an organizing metaphor even for a problem that appears to need a solution outside the ordinary. The platform found a formal representation in the organizational chart of Olivetti Systems & Networks, the main operating company under the new arrangement, and was understood by management in the first instance as a deployment able to offer potentialities that were analogous to those of computer platforms. The individual *components* of the organizational platform represented the well-known arrangements: departments, functions, divisions. Each so defined unit increased its clarity of mission and facilitated reporting and control at least at a local level. The *integration* of the different components was flexible and could not be read from the organizational chart alone. Depending upon the technological mission, functions like R&D, which were repositories of generic competencies, could be recombined towards the goal of the moment (market-driven applications, firmware, data communications, etc.). Operations were shaped concurrently to serve the new markets. Integration also dealt with units and organizations outside the boundaries of Olivetti. Thus, venture capital, joint R&D projects, and global alliances would be set up and dismantled according to circumstances. Correspondingly, the relationship between R&D and the marketing function was tightened. Development was more closely geared to marketing: sales forecasts and marketing evaluations for a new product were swiftly transferred and hardwired into computer platforms.

Computer platforms and their shortened life cycle tended to result in industry leaders that prevailed only temporarily and for one product: for example, Compaq had been the early leader for the Intel 386 platform, while Olivetti arrived among the first with the 486 family. Computer vendors exchanged the best motherboards and cards through OEM agreements and other forms of alliances aimed at cutting development time and time to market, and maximizing volume. Such agreements and alliances lasted only for the product life cycle, one chip generation, and, as a result, the industry itself could be looked at as a modular platform, in the sense that a vendor could avail itself of many small and large suppliers for the different standardized components. These are then assembled in a unique product: a standardized platform with a certain number of add-ons and features.

A second clue comes from the very recombination processes, which give dynamism to the plastic configuration of the platform in response to environmental changes. High-tech firms must cope frequently with kaleidoscopic change, where a small, apparently insignificant variation can dramatically alter the entire action set (the task, the market, the business) of the organization. Growth patterns are volatile, it is hard to capitalize on early success, periodic readjustments will not do, and crises cannot be solved once and for all. In such an environment the firm must exhibit a variety of flexible responses: ability to react quickly; resilience in the face of disturbances; and being capable of facing radical surprises, the necessary consequence of chaotic change. The platform organization can be seen as the arrangement most suited to cope with chaotic environments, where sudden events can tilt established patterns of identity, organization, culture, routines, and capabilities.

The power of junk and *shih*

Organizational structures can be compared on the basis of their efficiency in dealing with transaction costs. The multidivisional form, the matrix, or the network should be selected for their relative ability to coordinate businesses at the lowest cost. This efficiency perspective, however, assumes implicitly that the technology of products and processes remains relatively stable, so that there is time to set up a new structure, fine tune it, and evaluate its results; that is, if the technology and the task are known and stable, one can engage in exercises of vertical integration versus market externalization, and then compare the results at the margin. In the industries where Olivetti operates, however, the rules of the game are different. We enter the world of dynamic technologies: it is hard to tell what operating system will prevail in two years' time, or what chip architecture will be the industry standard. Firms are uncertain about the technology trajectory they are on, and consequently about their industry and business identity. Whenever perceptions change, the very business mission and primary task can shift abruptly too: was Olivetti in PCs or platforms; a low-cost manufacturer or a systems integrator? In such a turbulent context, plans to integrate vertically or demerge in order to lower transaction costs miss the point. The issue may not be whether to integrate or not, as much as with whom, in what industry: with a telecom company, a chip maker, a large software vendor, a media company, or a mix of these? Theories that prescribe how to set up efficient organizational structures around a complex primary task lose part of their relevance, for one cannot know in advance the complexity of the task, nor its precise nature and contours. Specifically, analysing and evaluating the platform organization at a fixed point in time is of little use: it may look like a matrix, or a functional hierarchy, and one may wonder how well its particular form fits the market for that period and what its level of efficiency really is. What should be appreciated, instead, is the whole sequence of forms adopted over time, and the speed and friction in shifting from one to the other. A useful way to look at the platform organization may be as a string: that is, the sequence of forms it is able to display, and the temporal links between them. The platform can be looked at longitudinally, as a bundle of trajectories punctuated by stations. At each station, one may find a familiar organizational structure (the matrix, the network, etc.) that somehow does the job, usually in an inefficient way, for circumstances keep changing and leave little time for optimization. And there are tracks: riding on them means that the organization members change their formative context while passing through instabilities, turmoil, experimentation, and doubts about structures, design criteria, technologies, missions, and identities. The platform organization retains all of this: the static and dynamic mechanisms, the certainties and the doubts, the visions and their smashing, the ready-made junk routines and the not-yet-made ones.

How do top managers take the organization from one station to another along the trajectories which define its evolving business identity? In other words, how do managers go about the job of recombining structures? The Olivetti case shows rather vividly that in the computer industry strategic management mainly consists of placing bets on what will be its next primary task; all the other choices, such as alliances and vertical integration, follow the provisional outcome of such gambles. The platform, being reconfigurable, is particularly suited to supporting the practice of betting and the high flexibility entailed in exiting when one is losing, or moving in rapidly to reap the benefits of the moment, or adapting to the new circumstances that require a new risky move. Betting can hardly be planned in advance. Something deeper is involved at each turn, especially if the previous turn has been successful: the identity of the business may have changed as an outcome of a particular gamble, so that past experience is of little use. The platform is a context that allows for such opportunistic, semi-blind strategic decision making: its identity and mission are allowed to drift in order to stay open to networking with the most appropriate constellation of partners required at each moment. Because of its fuzziness and inter-twined structure the platform seems to defy any attempt to make sense of standard approaches to gaining a competitive edge. On the one hand, the platform organization upsets such prescrip-tions, because it looks hybrid, blurred, and often stuck betwixt and between. On the other, it can be swiftly set up to respond to a competitor's move according to the rules of competitive advantage. It is chameleonic: if Olivetti were facing a threat by NCR, rather than Compaq, it could rearrange its internal resources in order to sport the appropriate competitive stance, and stage an attack against the specific rival or class of firms. Indeed, one of the striking characteristics of the platform con-sists in being programmed for perpetual transformation, for gen-erating organizational arrangements, cognitive frames, and for constantly branching out to other, radically different businesses, identities, and industries.

Managers as improvisers

How do managers operate in such a complex and elusive organ-izational context?

The unpredictability caused by the strategic betting, the mimetic behaviour, and the sedimentation of arrangements due to the ineradicable inertia of pre-existing routines and structures all conjure to present the platform as a generic context, full of junk organizational routines that can be harnessed depending upon the needs of the moment. Traditional organizations, even the newer forms, come with a bundle of requirements and expectations that create a reference context for managerial action. In the platform organization managers have to enact the context while they act, make choices, and envision strategies. In conventional organizations the landscape is given, and management is the foreground figure. In the platform, background landscape and foreground actions are painted both simultaneously and disjointedly, each giving meaning to the other in the process.

Managers have to adopt multiple standards in order to move around the redundant parts of the platform. They may have to behave according to a hierarchical context (arrangement and attitude) in some parts of the organization, or as network operators (again both organizationally and cognitively) in the network setting. The platform is a meta-organizational context that creates multiple dependencies and belongings. While in a matrix a manager reports to two or more bosses, in the platform a manager may operate within two or more organizational forms at the same time. Note that such a meta-organizational context is not fully designed; rather it emerges as the result of the managers' situated rationalities and actions, while they recombine artfully those very arrangements, and operate within them reproducing a logic, such as the recombination process, that can be invoked once more. Managers as *bricoleurs* and improvisers stay creative in the face of surprises, because they are accustomed to operate in disordered conditions and somehow pull order out of the resources and routines to hand.

In sum, the platform is far from being a new, distinct organizational structure, where one can recognize a fresh configuration of authority and communication lines. Rather, it is a virtual and collective cognitive scheme, expressed through actions of recombination, that governs, and is supported by, the bedrock of practices of a community: a pool of human resources, described in the Olivetti case as the old boys' network at the top management level. The platform resembles a *habitus* (Bourdieu 1977) unique to Olivetti top management, composed of organizing principles such as betting, opportunistic deployment of partnerships, pragmatism, fast learning from the technological architectures, and so on. These principles are rerun in the heads of managers and surface in their acts of improvisation: being shared collectively, they maintain coherence in an organization where structures are continuously eroded.

A concluding picture

The main performance characteristics of the platform can be synthesized as follows:

- it allows the coexistence at the level of organizational architecture of a multiplicity of structures: managers remain capable, regardless of context, of applying a wide range of different responses to surprises;
- it allows an easy transfer of frames and routines across disparate organizational settings;
- it allows multiple modes of resource utilization: managers, far from being influenced by the extant organizational context, are able to reinterpret *ex novo* given resources in terms of frames that may differ significantly from those that led to the acquisition of those very resources;
- it coexists with unpredictability: formulation and implementation of plans are carried out in a traditional fashion but the platform's *habitus* is manifested when facing surprises and often leads to the unexpected utilization of existing resources;

- it achieves flexibility by lashing together structures that have a high potential for action in response to chaotic events (*shih*), rather than maximizing efficiency around stable tasks and technologies.

Its global technology strategy has been vital for Olivetti and has produced an array of moves and organizational interventions that made Olivetti a network firm during the study period. However, strategy and the resulting organization emerged implicitly rather than being determined at the outset. Although management and industry observers tend to give a systematic, *ex post* reconstruction, where each step of the technology strategy finds precise reasons and justifications, I suggest that, behind the charts shown on the official transparencies, what prevailed was a pragmatic muddling through, turning and reacting nimbly, as circumstances changed and opportunities became disclosed. Even when there were precise goals and plans, for example in setting up specific alliances and acquisitions, these did not meet their targets: surprises appeared instead. Evaluating the success or failure of strategic moves by the attainment of the goals for which they were originally set up misses the point. What does matter is the process, its stations and tracks: often, the sheer engaging in such moves has contributed to push Olivetti along newly emerging technology trajectories. Furthermore, attention to the role of surprises reveals that the organizational outcome of the technology strategy in action, as opposed to the one formally espoused, is a pasted-up organization where elements of the old are intertwined with trials of the new. The overall picture is a fuzzy organization, which differs from the formal charts, no matter how frequently they are updated, and which is sufficiently responsive to the new. In such a context, learning from surprises turns out to be a valuable core capability, just as much as being able to analyse technologies and the competition. In order to capture such emerging qualities, we cannot rely on traditional organizational models, or even on newer ones such as the network firm. They all suffer from the fact of being too tidy, pre-planned, too good to be true, given the high levels of uncertainty management have to face.

In response, we have introduced the metaphor of the platform. On the surface it appears to be a resilient pool of junk resources, badly organized according to efficiency criteria, but these resources are available for deployment when the technology strategy requires it. On a deeper level it is a collective cognitive scheme that allows managers to try out, relentlessly, new organizational combinations.

We have placed the disturbing confusion that permeated Olivetti's internal organization at the centre of the theoretical notion of platform, while the chart in which Olivetti was pictured as a network firm is taken just as a cleansed *ex post* account.

Is it possible to systematize the way of operating of the platform organization, to find a detailed theoretical model, or even any underlying laws, for such a happenstance organization? Can strategic tinkering be governed? Once again, the analogy with architecture may suggest a positive answer. Deconstructivist buildings-as-landscapes obtain movement through the artful display of shifting masses, collapsing solids, juxtaposed and twisted volumes. They seem to disregard the rules established by modern architecture, but still they stand stubbornly solid and make a unitary stylistic statement over their environment, precisely because behind their deceptive disorder lies a deeply thought-out answer to some of the canonical problems of architecture.

The platform, with its emphasis on fragmentation, fuzziness, and displacement, should not be discarded, even by those who enact it, as the inevitable outcome due to environmental uncertainty and imperfections in the formal organization. Rather, it should be appreciated as a necessary culture bed for experimentation and recombination, providing the decision maker with an almost infinite variety of elements (frames, visions, mechanisms, and arrangements) to compose new pro-tem solutions faster and more efficiently. Management in high-tech firms ought to admit that their job in coping with technological discontinuities is not to make decisions at the centre of a network firm; rather what they do is to tinker at the periphery of that pasted-up organizational platform they constantly enact. Being smart improvisers makes business sense, especially when business itself appears to make very little sense.

8

Kairos (and *Affectio*)

Turbulent economic times seem to put improvisation at the centre stage of business management and organization studies, and not exclusively in the high-tech industries described in the previous chapter. Globalization, with its related risks and widespread side effects stemming from large-scale activities and systems, makes the highly situated process of improvisation a valued intervention. This activity is needed to fill the gaps of planning, cope with unexpected consequences, and, in general, face emergencies. Weick (1993) has shown in his vivid account of the Mann Gulch fire disaster how improvisation can be an antidote to panic and, more generally, to those forces, whether natural or psychological, that can bring about the collapse of sense making and organization. Also, more common activities like making choices on a market show many of the characteristics of improvisation. Thus, Hayek (1945) is unsurpassed in

An earlier version of this chapter was published as C. U. Ciborra (1999) 'Notes on improvisation and time in organizations', *Accounting, Management and Information Technologies*, 9: 77–94.

interpreting the price system as a way of coordinating local, highly situated decisions made on the spur of the moment by market agents. Even within hierarchical work organizations, several studies have shown the highly ad-hoc character of many actions in coping with events and situations that do not fit immediately the planned, hierarchical procedures (see for example Suchman 1987; Brown and Duguid 1991).

Improvisation can be looked at as a special case of situated action, highly contingent upon emerging circumstances; unifying design and action; quick, sudden, and extemporaneous. Note that, nowadays, improvisation, like situated action, is seen from a privileged standpoint—the one of cognition: a problem needs to be solved in the context of emerging circumstances, on the spur of the moment. Improvising is usually linked to the exploitation of tacit knowledge. Collective improvisation is discussed within the framework of distributed cognition (Hutchins 1996).

In one word, the prevailing cognitive study of improvisation concludes that any entity that can reasonably be thought of as planning or executing action can also be thought of as improvising. But, if improvisation is just quick problem solving that takes into account emerging circumstances by some sort of ongoing feedback on the very design of the action being undertaken, then the critique of Vera and Simon (1993) to the whole situated action paradigm applies to it too. The latter authors ask, 'what's new, or so special?' In principle, when reconstructing improvised decision making, symbolic representations of the ongoing problem space can be drawn, algorithms can be identified, problem solving programmes can be written, which include the stuff of which AI is made: plans; if-then-elses; means–ends chains etc. But, once improvisation gets analysed as quick design and simultaneous implementation of plans of action, factoring early feedback from execution, where has its magic gone? Can such an analysis offer anything new or alternative to the prevailing managerial and systems models that put at the centre of their discourse information, knowledge modelling, and planning?

To overcome such an impasse we need to step back and revisit the intellectual roots of situated action, of which we consider improvisation as a special case, in phenomenology.

Improvisation as situated action

Improvisation is currently treated in the management and organization literatures as a form of situated action where the emphasis is placed on its temporal dimension and its description is largely based on a cognitive perspective. Thus, improvisation is an activity where composition and execution, thinking and doing, converge in time or occur simultaneously.

Key aspects of such a form of thinking in the midst of the action are:

- the focus of attention being on emerging circumstances and current conditions;
- intuition guiding action where no script seems to be in control: improvisation has little to do with scripted plans;
- on the spot surfacing, restructuring, and testing of intuitive understanding;
- solving a problem with no preconception of how to do it beforehand;
- situational decision making.

This short list shows how definitions may vary in their attempts to grasp selected aspects of the phenomenon. But they share a common approach, the cognitive perspective, and a common understanding of the temporal dimension: quick, simultaneous, and on the spur of the moment.

There is a situation, and it is emergent: the trick of improvisation, as opposed to scripting and planning, is to capture in the emergent problem solving all the latest circumstances. Thus, improvisation is about compiling scripts on the fly and problem solving on the spur of the moment, and so on. But, no matter what the specific description, it is, after all, about problem solving, scripting, and thinking.

Regarding the temporal dimension, do not be misled by 'improvised' enquiries into the root of the word, such as the opposite of the Latin word *proviso*, i.e. not stipulated beforehand, or *improvisus*, meaning not seen ahead of time. The fact is that there was no Latin noun that means improvisation having its roots in 'improv . . .'. The phrase used in Latin was instead: *extemporalis actio*. This term is still used today and one of the adjectives most frequently adopted to describe improvisation both in music (jazz) and managerial literature is indeed 'extemporaneous'. Also, the managerial literature seems to be concerned with the simultaneity of different activities, such as thinking and doing, and the speed of knowing and acting: for example, to discover a way to do a 22-second information search in 2 seconds. But does extemporaneous mean just fast and simultaneous? It does not. Etymologically it means outside of time, or outside the normal flow of time. Interestingly, the literature mentioned above takes no notice of this, and Weick (1998) rightly points out that if speed is the main characteristic of this activity, then in many circumstances coping with a faster tempo would condemn the agent to using pre-planned, repetitive procedures to keep the performance going. In other words, higher speed may encourage, not improvisation, but a sudden reversion back to old ideas and routines. We are, then, left with the conceptual inconsistency of improvisation being advocated for fast product development, prompt market decision making, and successful organizational performances, on the one hand, and on the other the very carrying out of such activities, which seem to require simplification, accelerated production, less slack, forcing people back on older tracks and away from adaptive improvisation. In sum, gaining speed may undermine spontaneity and extemporaneity.

The cognitive view of improvisation is rooted into, and echoes very closely, the earlier study of situated action vs. planning carried out by Suchman (1987). In her work, the situation is defined as the full range of resources that the actor has available to convey the significance of his or her action and to interpret the actions of others. Specifically, in analysing how employees deal with photocopiers that break down, she suggests that 'the situation of the user comprises preconceptions about the nature of the machine and the operations required to use it, combined with moment by moment interpretations of evidence found in and through the actual course of its use' (1987). Note the ingredients of the theory of improvisation. On the cognitive side they are preconceptions, interpretations, and evidence; and the temporal dimension is moment by moment. 'Action is contingent on a complex world of objects, artefacts and other actors located in space and time. And this is an essential resource that makes knowledge possible and gives action its sense' (Suchman 1987). Thus, the situated action paradigm states the importance of fleeting circumstances on which the making sense of the action relies, but which these accounts of action routinely ignore. Plans, while providing sense or meaning to an action through a formalized representation of events, resources, and interactions over (clock) time, do not help cope with unexpected breakdowns and more generally emerging circumstances.

But does all this really differ from the AI planning approach?

For the latter, a physical symbol system interacts with the external environment by receiving sensory stimuli that it converts into symbol structures in memory, and it acts upon the environment in ways determined by symbol structures. The memory is an indexed encyclopaedia, where representations of external situations are stored. Stimuli coming from the environment invoke the appropriate index entries. 'Sequences of actions can be executed with constant interchange among (a) receipt of information about the current state of the environment (perception), (b) internal processing of information (thinking), and (c) response to the environment (motor activity). These sequences may or may not be guided by long-term plans (or strategies that adapt to the feedback of perceptual information)' (Vera and Simon 1993). In other words, the proponents of the more traditional AI approaches based on representations and symbol processing argue that one can design and build symbol systems that continually revise their description of the problem space and the alternatives available to them. This mimics one of the key ideas of the situated action perspective, i.e. the importance of moment by moment capture of the full situation of action. Plans can be seen not just as symbolic representations of fixed sequences of actions, but as strategies that determine each successive action as a function of current information about the situation. Here we come full circle: the AI perspective coincides with the definition given above of improvisation as 'situational decision making'. They contain the same ingredients: symbols, goals, means and ends, plans and actions. They differ just in terms of high speed and fine adaptability.

What if, instead, the very view of situated action and improvisation as cognitive enterprises is the source of the impasse in the debate, and also the reason why the descriptions discussed so far are not able to address innovatively the issue of the temporal, or better the extra-temporal, dimension of improvisation?

Rediscovering the situation of the actor, in the situation

In phenomenology, interestingly enough, one can find at least four different terms for describing and interpreting a 'situation': *Stelle*, meaning position and place; *Lage* as condition and disposition; *Situation* (in German) as the culminating limit situation of making a choice; and last, but not least, *Befindlichkeit* (Heidegger 1962). It is precisely the latter term that can help us in opening new dimensions. It is derived from the common expression 'Wie befinden Sie sich', a courteous way to ask, 'How are you?' Thus, *Befindlichkeit* is the situation one finds oneself in. But what situation? The loose arrangements of resources in the environment? The emerging physical and social circumstances? Not at all: the expression refers to the existential situation of the actor. 'How do you *feel* today?' Thus, *Befindlichkeit* combines the idea of situatedness and of feeling and faring, of where and how one finds oneself.

Note how the German word captures the common way of enquiring about the situation of the people we encounter every day. So routine and ubiquitous a habit, yet still totally absent not only from the symbolic representations of human problem solving—that one would expect[1]—but also, and this is fatal, from

---

[1] Actually, Simon (1967) put forward an early exploration of emotions in a cognitive and AI perspective. He interprets emotions as 'interrupt mechanisms' needed by the human problem solver to switch programmes of action when facing radically new circumstances. These, because of their novelty, typically give rise to 'emotional responses'.

the situated action approaches. Indeed, both seem to consider the actor as a cognitive robot. The discussion is about how the robot solves the problems, learns about circumstances, and plans or reacts to emergent conditions. Later appeals to 'situated and embodied knowledges' still evade a reply to the ordinary question, the how-are-you of the actor, his moods, feelings, affections, and fundamental attunement with the situation. What is missing from the situated action literature is precisely an enquiry into the situation of the actor, specifically his moods.

Only by bringing back into the picture the situation of the actor, those fleeting personal circumstances (captured by the term 'mood'; in Latin, *affectio*), and not only the emerging environmental circumstances, can we get to a fresh understanding of improvisation, one that the mere cognitive perspective seems to be unable to deliver, except as a stale, *ex post* reconstruction of problem solving routines designed and acted on the spur of the moment.

Any actor enters into the situation with a mood that is elusive and can hardly be controlled, designed, or represented in symbols: fear, anxiety, happiness, panic, or boredom. Moods are the uncontrollable changing skies of the otherwise flat world of the appearances of cognition and action, whether planned or situated. Precisely because moods come and go like the weather: they are apparitions, very close to who we are in the situation. They are so ephemeral, sometimes superficial and unexplained, but they precede, or better ground, any mental representation of the situation and action strategy. But moods are far from being just private states. They disclose the world; they set the stage of our encounter with the world.

When we encounter the world in a situation, certain things, people, or circumstances matter. This 'mattering' is grounded in one's affectedness. Hence affectedness discloses the world *as* a threat, boring or exciting. It sets the stage, shaping problem definition, solving, design, and action. In other words, our being open and encountering the world, our being amidst people and circumstances, and the related intentional projects of action, planned or situated, are constituted within a fundamental attunement, the mood: moods can change, but we are never without one. In this respect, not only is symbolic representation not primary, neither is cognition. Note that if moods provide the ground in which our encountering the world and defining the situation take place, we can seldom choose such a ground: rather, we are thrown from it into the situation. Moods colour indelibly our being in the situation. Unless I am in a mood I will not be affected, touched, or interested by anything. Precisely, because a mood is not a mere consequence of our actions, its essence and origin tend to remain concealed. Moods are the fundamental ways in which we are disposed in such and such a state; they are not the direct consequence of our thinking, doing, and acting: they are rather the presupposition, the medium within which those activities take place. The most powerful moods attune us with the situation so strongly it almost seems there are no moods at all (and this is the trap into which even those who write about embodied knowledge seem to fall nowadays, by failing to put moods at the centre of attention).

To conclude, the way we *care* about the world unfolds according to the passing mood that attunes us with the situation. Intentionality, the reading or reregistering of circumstances that we perform either by planned or improvised action, the in-order-tos of projects, the selection of appropriate means to ends are all rooted in such a ground, our basic attunement. The study of situated action in general, and of improvisation in particular, has focused so far only upon the later stages of this process, on the

encounter between intentions and situations, but has systematically failed to reckon the (moody) situation of the actor.

Improvising as a mood

Looking at improvisation as a special disposition or attunement
with the situation, a special way of being amidst the world and
being thrown into it, opens up a different point of access to the
phenomenon: improvisation as mood. This complicates our
enquiry, though. Actions can be studied as the carrying out of
projects, plans, or intentions, or as emergent responses to circumstances, as the cognitive approaches (symbolic representation and plans or situated actions) show. As mentioned above,
instead, moods often cannot be forcibly brought about and are
not necessarily linked to a plan or an action: they are the ground
or the medium for them, but not the other way round. We slip
into them unaware. Hence it is difficult to make an attunement
into an object of cognitive analysis.

Let us then try to evoke the notion of improvisation as mood by
recounting the episode described and interpreted by Weick (1993)
in his study of the Mann Gulch fire disaster. Improvisation is what
allowed Dodge, the smokejumpers' captain, to rescue himself
when most of the rest of the team died in a suddenly exploding
forest fire in Montana (Maclean 1992). Dodge was able to invent
and implement on the spot a rescue procedure, consisting of burning the high grass in front of him with a match and throwing
himself into it. When the wall of the main fire, blown by the
wind, arrived, it passed over him because he had created a clear-
ing in which the fire could not find dry grass for fuel to continue
burning. It is a typical example of improvisation, since such
a procedure was not known or learnt (it became part of the

standard smokejumper training *after* that tragic episode). It is highly situated; it comes out of a reading of the situation at that very moment—high grass, matches, incoming firewall; it is quick—Dodge's fast reasoning led to the solution to the problem—the fire needs fuel, hence let's eliminate the fuel source. 'How do I do it?' Paradoxically, by creating a new fire, and so on. As usual, however, the *ex post* analysis of Dodge's skilful improvisation leaves the observer with a bitter aftertaste. Namely, after-the-fact analysis shows an ingenious problem solving strategy, artfully and promptly implemented. This strategy can be easily represented and reproduced so as to become a training routine. The time dimension seems to be straightforward: Dodge was quick in framing the problem, discovering a solution, and implementing it just in time. By the way, he was not in a hurry: after the first match he considered using another one. Once again, where is the difference from a planned action?

What gets lost in a cognitive perspective of situated action or symbolic representation, which makes Dodge's actions a true case of improvisation, is what happened to the other team members. They were running very close to Dodge; they were exposed to the very same situation; thanks to the wind lifting the clouds of smoke a couple of times, they could even see what he was doing. Dodge yelled at them to do the same or join him by jumping in his man-made fire, but apparently they could not hear what he was trying to communicate, because of the crackling noise of the incoming wall of fire. However, they failed to understand. Precisely because they could see what he was trying to achieve, they came to the conclusion that their captain was out of his mind and committing suicide, so they carefully avoided the provoked fire area, running into the high grass just next to it. They died within a few metres. This tragic outcome seems to defy any cognitive interpretation: distributed cognition worked against the

team members; the rescue routine was misread; the same situation (recall that the whole team was contained in a very small
area) did not lead to the same interpretation, design, and action.

Let us try to interpret the ways people encounter the situation,
and design and implement action as moody ways. What decided
the different outcomes, the opposite understandings, the alternative situated knowledges was not the situation, but the contrasting moods the actors were in. If the smokejumpers were just
cognitive robots, with more or less similar experience, once
exposed to the same situation they would have come up with similar answers, or be able to quickly imitate a rescue procedure
enacted by one member of the team. On the contrary, they were
all confronting a culminating, supreme situation. They were
spatially close but existentially far apart in respect to this supreme
situation: their fundamental attunements with the situation varied
greatly and their different moods affected distinctively their
understanding and ways of acting. The team members were
victims of panic, and in this fundamental mood they interpreted
what the captain was doing as 'going nuts' and an explicit
authorization by their captain for everyone to go mad. Panic
determined their experiencing lack of time and being over-
whelmed by the world, the forest on fire. Maclean (1992) colourfully describes Dodge's mood in the following way: 'Inside
Dodge there was the only cool spot in the total fire scene.' This
coolness is the secret engine of his capacity to improvise, to find
all the time that was needed to come up with a solution, though
paradoxical, and implement it.

The episode also suggests a new way of studying improvisation as mood, by contrasting it with other moods. But there are
many moods out there (around 400, the psychologists suggest, at
least in Western culture). Which ones to choose for this com-
parative exercise? As we have already remarked many times,

improvisation strikes us because of its sudden, extemporaneous, and full impact. That is why we should contrast it with affections characterized by their negligible or null effect and by their being sticky with clock time. Good candidates are of course panic, as shown above, and boredom. Both have problems in leading to any form of effective action and with the passing of clock time, though in different ways and for different reasons. Let us examine them in order.

Panic

Our existence unfolds by our relentless taking care of the world, usually encountered as an intricate web of interdependent tools, of ready at hand artefacts, resources, and people. This is how we are most of the time amidst the world. In this environment we develop and implement specific projects, made of sequences of in-order-tos, framed into plans, strategies, or immediate, almost unconscious reactions to emerging circumstances. When the fundamental attunement of panic sets in, this ordinary way of understanding and acting in the world stops. The world overwhelms us. It ceases to appear as a set of tools ready for use; we lack the time to implement our projects. Resources are not at hand; in particular, time is not available. We quickly come to inaction or engage frantically in whatever activity comes to hand, after having considered all possible options and jumped to the conclusion that none will be successful. Angst for the lack of time to pursue further exploration of alternatives blocks decision-making, which in its turn may lead to inaction or to the haphazard compulsive pursuit of an activity picked from those available in the situation, but with no really adaptable strategy. That our being-in-the-world is, from the moment of birth, permanently set towards death suddenly emerges as the only default alternative that has always been there, but which gets forgotten through being amidst the daily chores and care. Death sets in as the implicitly preferred choice, the only one that can calm down the highest levels of anxiety determined by panic.

This is the structure of panic as mood. Care is aimless. The world is unusable. Intentionality has nowhere to go except to consider the supreme alternative of death. Time is lacking. As the Mann Gulch accident shows vividly, entering the situation with the mood of panic tends to close off all alternatives: especially the invention and implementation of new ones. Even imitation, as a strategy of action, is impeded and falls victim to that mood.

Boredom

If panic implies that things, including time, matter too much (the world overwhelms us), in boredom nothing really matters: the world is indifferent and time never seems to pass. If in panic we fall victim to the world and time, in boredom we try to kill time while being immersed in a fog of indifference. Depending upon the acuteness of the mood, Heidegger (1995) distinguishes three main states of intensifying boredom: becoming bored by something specific (a train does not arrive and we are waiting at the station watching the clock and trying out all sorts of pastimes); being bored with something (a nice evening spent with friends—time flew—still, when we get back home, we feel bored); finally, profound boredom—one finds it boring.

Starting from the superficial ways in which we deal with boredom in everyday life, we can encounter the inextricable relation of this mood with time. At first, it is under the form of whatever pastime we engage in to overcome boredom; we pass the time in order to master it, because time becomes long in waiting for a train that is late. Even our superficial, ordinary way of coping with the first level of boredom, being bored by, leads us to time, to an understanding of how time resonates in the background of being in the situation of waiting. When we are bored, our attunement, our way of being-amidst, is characterized by being in a time that passes too slowly, amidst a world that does not offer many resources to fight the length of the time.

The second type of boredom has a less specific object. We recognize retrospectively that we were bored by an evening spent out. Still, when we were passing it we had fun: we never watched the clock. It seems at first a more superficial, fleeting type of boredom, but it is more profound. Precisely because no specific pastime was deployed during the evening, it is apparent that the whole evening was the pastime used to fight boredom before it even arose. By deciding to allow ourselves a specific period of time to go out and have fun with friends, we have given ourselves time intentionally dedicated to finding ways to pass the time. This mood is not triggered by a specific, apparent cause, nor is it tied to a specific event or situation, rather it seems to stem from our existence. Note how, by not experiencing the flow of time through spending the evening out, we make the whole evening a 'single stretched now'; 'Entirely present to the situation, we bring our time to a stand' (Heidegger 1995).

Finally, consider the more profound form of boredom, 'one finds it boring'. We are empty, we want nothing from the particular beings in the situation, we are elevated beyond the particular circumstances. The whole situation becomes indifferent. What is peculiar about the last form of boredom is that there is no pastime in sight. Time does not drag for us, neither do we make it stand still. Rather, one feels 'removed from the flow of time', indifferent to time, timeless. Yet indifference means all material and human beings withdraw in retrospect (the past), in every prospect (future), and in the current aspect (present). Thus, this profound indifference is linked to the whole time horizon; and beings as a whole refuse themselves to us. What is striking about this form of boredom is that all dimensions of time (clock time; past, future, the now, etc.) do not matter. There is no determinate time point when this boredom arises; we do not worry at all about the clock, as we do not worry about beings and the world; we are not annoyed by any 'stretched now', i.e. the time span during which this boredom holds us. Actually, the profound boredom 'can take hold of us in an instant like a flash of lightning'. Time is there but in an unarticulated unity that entrances us. It is not only beings that refuse themselves, but time itself, as the horizon for the manifestness of those very beings (Heidegger 1995).

The temporality of improvisation

Panic and lack of time, boredom in its various forms and passing the time, are intertwined. Passing the time creeps into our being bored, as lack of time fuels panic. These moods appear to be far from superficial or contingent upon special events. They are profoundly concentrated on us, our situation and time, which is not clock time, rather *our* time. In particular, we have seen that the more profound boredom becomes, the more it appears rooted 'in the time that we ourselves are' (Heidegger 1995).

The opposite of improvisation is not planned action, it is boredom (and sometimes panic). During the latter, unarticulated time and refusal of the world leads to inaction. On the other hand, we can look at the former as the 'moment of vision', as the look of resolute decision in which the full situation of action opens itself and keeps itself open to our initiative of reregistering, recombination, and intervention. The cognitive perspective focuses on how smart improvisers are able to quickly reregister the world and recombine resources. But this is possible only because suddenly the world, its resources, and people matter differently, so that they can be singled out and recombined anew. Here, quickness is far from implying rigidity and reversion to the already known. Improvisation is a particular mood which hosts the reconfiguration of the ground in which we encounter the world (and devise and carry out those projects and actions of the cognitive perspective). Before action and before design there is a human existence thrown into a range of possibilities. The mood situates you in respect to these possibilities, discloses some and conceals others. The ones revealed will matter and will be the object of the simultaneous design, planning, and actions of the improviser. Moods like fear, laughter, or boredom involve above all a self-revelation, a disclosure of oneself as caring for (or being indifferent to) people and things in some definite way. Improvisation is that moment of vision and self-revelation where all the possibilities linked to the being-in-the-situation emerge out of the fog of boredom. Improvisation is the antidote to panic and boredom because it is 'extemporaneous', i.e. it ruptures the way time entrances us in both situations, by being either completely missing, or totally undifferentiated. Improvisation is then rupture, or, as the conductor Pierre Boulez describes it in music, *Einbruch*. Only if such a temporal entrancement is ruptured do beings no longer refuse themselves; possibilities for action emerge, graspable in the situation, and give to the actor the chance of intervening in the midst of beings at the specific moment and in the specific circumstances. The extemporaneous moment of vision is not some now-point we simply observe or describe after the fact. What Dodge did was to have this decisive look at the fire, and then followed the decision to *be* fire thrown into fire.

We take exception, then, to the cognitive view according to which any entity capable of planning or executing can improvise.

In the new perspective evoked here, we can rephrase that cognitive science statement as follows: any entity existing, being able to reflect on its existence and endowed with moods, feelings, and emotions, is able to improvise.

Some final thoughts (and feelings)

The study of improvisation as situated action, carried out within the cognitive perspectives in common currency, leaves us somewhat disappointed. We can easily find in it all the ingredients of more routine, planned action: goals, selection of alternatives, design, problem solving, and execution. The temporal aspects of improvisation are left unexplained. Extemporaneity is reframed as simultaneity and quickness, which obviously it is not. Improvisation was described in Latin as neither quick nor unplanned: it was called *extemporalis actio*.

We have submitted that one reason for this lack of assistance may lie in the distorted way in which the cognitive approaches consider situatedeness: they omit consideration of the situation of the actor. Implicitly, they deal with the situation as a set of emerging circumstances, but consider the actor as a passionless, problem solving robot.

We can find shelter by going back to the origins of phenomenology, the philosophical line of thought that in the last century celebrated the notion of situatedness. In that philosophical tradition, moods capture the essence of the fleeting attunement of the actor with the situation. Moods are far from being a marginal, colourful add-on to our mentalistic explanations of how the actors behave in situations. They are the ground for our encountering the world; understanding and acting in the situation. There is no situated action without a mood when we deal with human beings rather than cognitive robots.

We have looked then at improvisation as mood. Moods are best accessed by evoking, awakening, and comparing them. As a consequence, improvisation has not been contrasted with plans and procedure, as is customary in the cognitive enquiries into this phenomenon, but with other moods, those of panic and boredom, dropping the usual counterpoising of improvisation and planning.

The contrast with the latter, and its relationship with time, has allowed us to come closer to the meaning of the original definition of improvisation as an extemporaneous activity. In order to explain extemporaneity we have to go through the moods of the actor in a situation as linked to Heidegger's (1962) basic idea about the intimate coincidence of existence and time.

Our existential perspective has a number of further implications. Three can be mentioned, if only in passing. First, improvisation as moment of vision and disclosedness toward decision is much rarer than perhaps appreciated so far. Many forms of improvisation appear as pastimes against boredom. Few are actually antidotes to panic in emergencies. Second, if we accept Heidegger's (1995) statement according to which profound boredom defines the modern condition, a nocturnal light is cast on the last sixty years of management and organization science. Emphasis placed on programming, planning, and rational choice possibly conceals what goes on most of the time in most organizations for most people: boredom. Emphasis on decision making has entranced us and distracted us from appreciating that important decisions occur very seldom, while what prevails are all sorts of pastimes (programmes, methods, models) that punctuate colourfully the life of the workers and managers. Finally, computer systems increase the speed of activities and help in accelerating product development or, as we have seen, reducing the search for information from 22 to 2 seconds, but still we seem to continue to lack time, and behave more frantically than ever. Despite all such innovations, have we fallen victims of (clock) time as never before? Authentic extemporaneity eludes us in a world where scientific publications dedicated to celebrating it fake it as velocity. Alas, it is fast, it is digital: still one is bored.

Methodological Appendix (*Odos*)

Once a US colleague asked me, after reading some of the original papers included in this book, 'How do you come up with all these ideas, and are able to write such surprising papers?' Besides being obviously flattered, I found the question puzzling: I had never reflected systematically about the process by which the papers were generated. Since then I have tried to be on the alert, and to reflect a bit more each time I was concocting a new paper. I soon began to notice recursive patterns, especially in the rhetoric and the underlying message and flavour. But nothing about the commonalities underlying the process appeared to be sufficiently deep or focused to be put in writing. This was until I reread, for the *n*th time, the introduction to Heidegger's *Being and Time* (1962), specifically his definition of phenomenology. That definition (or rather my interpretation of it) at last helped me to make explicit the way that I understand how I proceed. To be sure, I have crafted such method in a dilettante fashion, along the way so to speak, starting from when I studied the global technology strategy of Olivetti, in the second half of the 1980s and came up with the idea of the platform organization endowed with *shih*.

The unveiling of the platform organization required a different analytical approach from the one common in industrial

The ideas for this chapter were laid out in C. U. Ciborra (1996), 'The platform organization: recombining strategies, structures and surprises', *Organization Science*, 7/2 (Mar.–Apr.): 103–18.

organization research, especially. New organizational forms like the network corporation were usually explained by referring to established concepts in organization theory, business policy, industrial economics, and information theory. Though different in perspective, all these disciplinary explanations shared the same basic assumptions: there are goals that guide the agents' decisions, there is a complex problem to be solved or a task to be executed; a corresponding strategy is deployed to achieve the goals and solve the problem; and a new structure is put in place to implement the solution. Hence, unitary, multidivisional, matrix, or networked organizational structures were regarded by scholars and practitioners as the rational responses to enable such moves. To be sure, decision makers would admit that day-to-day management is run in a more organic, ad-hoc fashion, and that textbooks and journal articles seldom seem to capture the intertwining of market events and managerial responses. They, especially in their *ex post* rationalizations, would also willingly admit to using schemes and models, such as the network, derived from studies of business organization and competitive analysis. The gap between what theoretical, *ex post* explanations and models can deliver and the actual garbage-can style of managerial choice is considered to be a fact of life by practitioners, and an unavoidable result of the limitations of any modelling approach by scholars. In order to allow the new concept of the platform organization to emerge I then took an alternative approach. First, the typical difficulties which appear when one endeavours to reconcile business practices with the actual choices in strategy formulation and structural design were attributed more to a basic inadequacy of the conceptual models, than to a supposedly natural divide between theory and practice, knowledge and action. Second, using first-hand evidence from the deployment of Olivetti's global technology strategy, I came to the conclusion that organizational models tend to focus only on snapshots of a complex, evolutionary process. This may be one of the reasons why observers and competitors who relied on those models were constantly puzzled by Olivetti's improvised moves. Snapshots can be relevant for actors and scholars to make sense of a complex process, and provide reference for *ex post* reconstruction of what happened. On the other hand, they represent postcards which can barely capture, let alone help interpret and explain, the forces behind the constant e-volution, re-volution, and de-volution of managerial action. Moreover, since such postcards were repeatedly relied upon and used by management when recounting events and rationalizing choices, they became silently embedded into scholarly interpretations and theories. Actions, or rather rationalizations of actions, and theories reinforced each other and became seemingly natural explanatory frames. They were retrieved when facing events or explaining phenomena, but also reproduced a self-sealing blindness to the new and the extant. As a consequence, I could only find the limits of current models and interpretations, and the roots of alternative ones, by reading between the lines of the stylized explanations; and peering into their wrinkles and especially into the interstices between practice, ongoing interpretations, and what was left out, or explained away by referring to the obvious background that both business practitioners and researchers were supposed to share. So far I have described my original dilettante approach.

My understanding of Heidegger's phenomenological method helped me to specify, and somewhat systematize, what I was (and am) doing. When approaching an organizational phenomenon we encounter at least two distinct forms of evidence. First, we are ready to deploy a set of ideas and models taken for granted in the domain of organization theories or consulting models. These ideas and models come almost to be identified with the phenomenon we want to grasp, or at least they provide an unquestioned context in which to grasp it. The study of Olivetti showed a first typology of such ideas and models very quickly taken for granted. These are the appearances in common currency in organizational and management studies: for example, the idea of the network firm as the outcome of the dense web of alliances enacted by high-tech companies. This model is the result of abstracting the actual moves and performances of companies. It becomes another organizational form, like the hierarchy or the matrix, endowed with essence and existence. Empirical, possibly quantitative, research activities can then be unleashed to go out there and measure the frequency and features of such a new form. Soon the idea of the network firm becomes a phenomenon whose existence is taken for granted. Scholars talk about it; special issues of journals are dedicated to it, not to mention the many seminars and conferences. Wide hospitality on PowerPoint slide presentations by consultants and practitioners is *de rigueur*. The phenomenon has become a fully-fledged appearance.

But out there, in the field, one often comes across a second range of taken for granted phenomena, very complementary to these appearances. While finding a new form, and having reified it, fills our methodological space with something to measure, the second type of phenomena points to a void, a vacuum that cannot be filled by any model, and it is thanks to such a vacuum that the new organizational form can emerge in a distinctive way. The vacuum is what disappears and cannot be captured and represented, but only alluded to thanks to utterances such as 'You know no organizational model will fully capture the actual flow of events', or 'The strategy was well laid out, but then, as you know, life is interesting because it is full of surprises', or 'We had to cross bridges when we encountered them!', or simply 'You know what I mean'. These everyday ways of speaking point to a shared, tacit, and taken for granted background between the researcher-interviewer and manager-interviewee. Such a background is crucial in providing the basis for a common understanding of questions and replies, but also to host the unexpressed aspects of organizational life, which will never make it through checklists or, even worse, questionnaires. However, the more this background is shared, not made an object of attention, and so self-evident as to be elusive, the more it hides something fundamental, albeit hidden on the surface, that should attract our attention and study. The turns of phrase just mentioned are performed when something odd has to be justified or dismissed. It is usually about the failure of the ideal models to capture the ongoing, observed flow of events. These expressions are then necessary to smooth out the reconstruction and the sense making of the events in the world constructed by formal models and methods. Still, that we have to indulge in such performances signals that there are apparitions that we need to spend some work on, in order to accommodate them somehow.

Following Heidegger, we can refer to the first type of evidence as illusory appearances. They usually attract our scientific attention. For example, the notion of the network firm, which captures the interest of scholars keen to find and study forms alternative to the hierarchy, works in reality as a show stopper, a model that biases, deflects, and ultimately blocks reflection. It synthesizes abruptly a chaotic organizational process, made of uncertainty in weaving alliances, their sudden upturns and failures, the surprises and drifting, especially during implementation. To be sure, companies engage in building webs of alliances and thus they mutate their structure and functioning. But we should deal with notions such as the network firm as having an extremely uncertain ontological status, a first appearance, and not the final outcome. A more promising attitude from the research standpoint would be to consider such appearances as what the phenomenon under investigation is *not*, although, or perhaps precisely because, everybody is talking about them.

The second type of evidence refers to those apparitions that sometimes break into the field study, the interview, the meeting, during those moments of truth that occur rarely but only at significant turns during fieldwork. Apparitions can be observed or reported. They deal with the *bricolage* and improvisation that people have to implement to find fixes to the plans and deal with surprises; the artistic touch sported in some moves; the intuition expressed even in the most high-tech environment; the celebration of the role of serendipity; and so on. All these practices become an indistinct background noise made of stories, innuendoes, or allusions. In the foreground, by contrast, the icy clarity of the model can emerge. The everyday apparitions should instead be looked at as symptoms, pointers to an organizational phenomenon that does not manifest itself directly. Both appearances and apparitions are generated by the underlying phenomenon to be unveiled. In Chapter 7 on *shih* the unveiling delivers the elusive phenomenon of Olivetti as an organizing platform. In particular, the study of breakdowns and how people react to surprises can help in disclosing the continuity and generativity of the thick texture that constitutes the taken for granted of organizational life. During breakdown, even if it is a crucial or fatal moment, the organizational routines lose their everyday meaning; business is not as usual and some decisive intervention is required in the light of the emerging circumstances. Improvised interventions tell us much about where the organization and its members are coming from and what they are being projected into, besides what keeps the routines, people, and meanings humming.

A final example is given by the special way Heidegger (1995) comes to approach the phenomenon of time. Here the appearance is clock time, to which most scientific endeavour refers. The apparitions are instead given, for example by the elusive moods, such as boredom, that reveal that time does not affect us just as neutral clock time. These moods, and the breakdowns they entail especially in the workings of pastimes, become as we saw in Chapter 8 on *kairos* the phenomenologist's privileged point of access to the question of what time is.

References

Beck, U. (1992), *Risk Society* (London: Sage).

Benveniste, E. (1969), *Le Vocabulaire des Institutions Indo-européennes* (Paris: Les Éditions de Minuit).

Bourdieu, P. (1977), *An Outline of a Theory of Practice* (Cambridge: Cambridge University Press).

Brown, J. S., and Duguid, P. (1991), 'Organizational learning and communities-of-practice: toward a unified view of working, learning and innovation', *Organization Science*, 2/1 (Feb.): 40–57.

Ciborra, C. U. (1996), 'What does groupware mean?', in C. U. Ciborra (ed.), *Groupware and Teamwork* (Chichester: John Wiley).

——*et al.* (2001), *From Control to Drift* (Oxford: Oxford University Press).

——and Lanzara, G. F. (1994), 'Formative contexts and information technology: understanding the dynamics of innovation in organizations', *Accounting, Management and Information Technologies*, 4/2: 61–86.

Darbon, S. (1997), 'La Grande Famille du rugby', *Communications*, 65: 49–58.

De Certeau, M. (1998), *The Practice of Everyday Life* (Berkeley and Los Angeles: University of California Press).

Derrida, J. (1997), *De l'Hospitalité* (Paris: Calmann-Lévy).

Giddens, A. (1990), *The Consequences of Modernity* (Oxford: Polity Press).

Hayek, F. A. (1945), 'The use of knowledge in society', *American Economic Review* (Sept.): 519–30.

Heidegger, M. (1962), *Being and Time* (New York: Harper & Row).

——(1978), 'The question about technology', in *Basic Writings* (London: Routledge).

——(1992), *Gelassenheit* (Stuttgart: Neske).

Heidegger, M. (1994), *Bremer und Freiburger Forträge* (1949; Frankfurt a.M.: Klostermann).

——(1995), *The Basic Concepts of Metaphysics: World, Finitude, Solitude* (Bloomington: Indiana University Press).

Husserl, E. (1970), *The Crisis of the European Sciences and Transcendental Phenomenology* (Evanston, Ill.: Northwestern University Press).

Hutchins, E. (1996), *Cognition in the Wild* (Cambridge, Mass.: MIT Press).

Jullien, F. (1995), *The Propensity of Things* (Cambridge, Mass.: Zone Books).

Kant, I. (1972), *Perpetual Peace: A Philosophical Essay* (London: Garland).

Latour, B. (1999), *Pandora's Hope: Essays on the Reality of Science Studies* (Cambridge, Mass.: Harvard University Press).

Maclean, N. (1992), *Young Men and Fire* (Chicago: University of Chicago Press).

Mintzberg, H. (1990), 'The design school: reconsidering the basic premises of strategic management', *Strategic Management Journal*, 11: 171–95.

Norman, D. A. (1988), *The Design of Everyday Things* (New York: Basic Books).

Schöen, D. A. (1983), *The Reflective Practitioner* (New York: Basic Books).

Schumpeter, J. A. (1950), *Capitalism, Socialism, and Democracy*, 3rd edn. (New York: Harper & Row).

Scott Morton, M. S. (ed.) (1991), *The Corporation of the 1990s* (Oxford: Oxford University Press).

Scribner, S. (1984), 'Studying working intelligence', in B. Rogoff and J. Lave (eds.), *Everyday Cognition* (Cambridge, Mass.: Harvard University Press).

Simon, H. A. (1967), 'Motivational and emotional controls of cognition', *Psychological Review*, 74: 29–39.

Suchman, L. (1987), *Plans and Situated Actions: The Problem of Human–Machine Communication* (New York: Cambridge University Press).

Sun-Tzu (1993), *The Art of Warfare* (New York: Ballantine).

Vera, A. H., and Simon, H. A. (1993), 'Situated action: a symbolic representation', *Cognitive Science*, 17: 7–48.

von Hofmannsthal, H. (1995), *The Lord Chandos Letter* (London: Syrens).

Weick, K. E. (1979), *The Social Psychology of Organizing* (Reading, Mass.: Addison Wesley).

——(1993), 'The collapse of sensemaking in organizations: the Mann Gulch disaster', *Administrative Science Quarterly*, 38 (Dec.): 628–52.

——(1998), 'Improvisation as a mindset for organizational analysis', *Organization Science*, 9/5: 543–55.

Winograd, T., and Flores, F. (1987), *Understanding Computers and Cognition: A New Foundation for Design* (Norwood, NJ: Ablex).

Index